My Kingdom is Not of This World

Mary Marriott

Mary Marriott

Kingdom Publishers

www.kingdompublishers.co.uk

My Kingdom is Not of This World

Copyright© Mary Marriott

All rights reserved. No part of this book may be reproduced in any form by photocopying or any electronic or mechanical means, including information storage or retrieval systems, without permission in writing from both the copyright owner and the publisher of the book. The right of Mary Marriott to be identified as the author of this work has been asserted by her in accordance with the Copyright, Designs and Patents Act 1988 and any subsequent amendments thereto.
A catalogue record for this book is available from the British Library.
All Scripture Quotations have been taken from the King James Version of the Bible

ISBN: 978-1-911697-18-3

1st Edition by Kingdom Publishers
Kingdom Publishers
London, UK.

You can purchase copies of this book from any leading bookstore or email contact@kingdompublishers.co.uk

Mary Marriott

Dedicated to the Glory of God

Mary Marriott

CONTENTS

REPENTANCE	9
THAT ONE DAY A WEEK	23
THERE IS ONLY ONE TRUTH	33
HE SUPPLIES ALL OUR NEEDS	41
RIGHTEOUSNESS AND SELF RIGHTEOUSNESS	52
FORGIVENESS AND UNFORGIVENESS	68
BLASPHEMY	78
TEMPTATION	87
WHAT IS THE PURPOSE OF LIFE?	95
BE STILL AND KNOW THAT I AM GOD	106
ONE HOUR AND THE TEN COMMANDMENTS	117
LONELINESS	134

Mary Marriott

REPENTANCE

What is repentance? Has the word become another 'disregard'? Has it been tossed aside? Has its familiarity become boring? Do we say, yes, I have repented; I am sorry for my sins; I am now getting on with my life; I say my prayers; I read the Scriptures; I go to church; I pay my tithes; I love God; I love my neighbour; Yes, I'm a good Christian?

That is wonderful – the criteria expected of a born again Christian is fulfilled.

However....

To repent of our sins for salvation is one thing, but to carry this repentance through is another. We have to continue to live in the way that God expects, and demands, of us.

The world stealthily crept into the church many years ago, surreptitiously doing its job, unseen, unrecognised, unfelt, by Christians. Satan is a sneak, taking advantage of the vulnerable, gullible and equable, working on them in this modern age, drawing more and more unsuspecting folk into His world, having them believe that all things are acceptable. But they are not. We are to be set apart from the world – be in, not of it. Let us not be naïve. Fornication for example. This is a word one very rarely hears mentioned. What does it mean?

It means having sex outside of marriage. Many think that because they love one another, 'and the greatest gift is love', it is all right to co-habit. Is it? Does God allow it? It might not be one of the Ten Commandments, but it is mentioned in Scripture. **Hebrews 13:4 Marriage is honourable among all, and the bed undefiled; but fornication and adulterers God will judge.**

As Christians we must heed our actions and look at ourselves and ask if we ever question co-habiting, or 'living together' as it is commonly known. It is admissible in the eyes of the world, but it certainly is, and should go without saying, a turning away from God.

We have to work on being perfect, and one way to begin is to examine our lives as Christians. The world looks at us, knowing that we are supposed to be different, but sees us as the same as they are - except for the fact that we go to church on Sundays, and think that we are better than they. We must remember that we are an example to others.

We are not to be self-righteous in our attitude, but by keeping to the rules, we remain safe, and so hopefully set a precedent to those alien to us.

Co-habiting is a very serious matter. We must wake up to this fact and look at it for what it is.

In the Old Testament, we understand that before the 'institution' of marriage, people were married when they first 'knew' their partner – the first time they had sexual intercourse.

Genesis 4:1 Now Adam knew his wife, and she conceived and bore Cain, and said, "I have acquired a man from the Lord."

In Genesis 24:67 Then Isaac brought her into his mother's tent, and he took Rebecca and she became his wife and he loved her.... If that was the case today, many will have been married over and over again!

Because marriage is considered to be sacred and a sacrament, it must be treated as such. Commitment is important and one must be genuine and serious in going into a relationship. It is binding.

When we ask Jesus to live in our lives, we make a promise to Him; the same goes for couples who love each other and want to spend the rest of their lives together. It is a massive decision to make, but once made it is to be honoured.

We are all sinners, but we need to be saved sinners – saved from the penalty of hell. We cannot just live our lives as we want in a worldly way, with all the attributes the world offers; we have to be different; we should want to be different.

We are so caught up with worldly attractions, the difference between us and them is hardly visible. We are blinded – 'there are non so blind as those who cannot see.'

It is the spiritual eyes with which we need to see our Christian behaviour. Our natural eyes naturally take in the things of the world, the fruits of temptation that pass in front of us daily. Being frail humans, we succumb easily, eager to taste forbidden fruits because sin is sweet, it is attractive. The snake strikes its venom. But when we use our spiritual eyes and look on the temptations, we will automatically see that they are moments in which we could be snared, and must take action to avoid.

Let us take a look at **John 17:14-17** where Jesus is praying to His Father for His disciples. **"I have given them Your word; and the world has hated them because they are not** of the world, just as I am not of the world. I do not pray that You should take them out of the world, but that You should keep them from the evil one. They are not of the world, just I am not of the world. Sanctify them by Your truth. Your word is truth."

Jesus is asking His Father to <u>sanctify</u> them by His Truth. (His Truth allows them to become holy.) This He does. And His prayer is still the same for us today.

'Sacred' comes from the word sanctify, and, when we speak of the 'sacrament' of marriage, we mean that marriage is 'sanctified' by God, made sacred, made holy; it is a sacrament.

Colossians 3:5 Put to death, therefore, whatever belongs to your earthly nature: sexual immorality, impurity, lust, evil desires and greed, which is idolatry.

Many find it difficult not to conform to the world. The 21st century offers us so much in the way of earthly desires. All the 'must-haves', and 'you deserve its', at times play havoc with our minds, but there is no need for this distress as we learn to focus on Him who regards this world as not His.

Jesus, Himself, says in **John 18** that "My Kingdom is not of this world". We need to ask ourselves if we really want what this worldly kingdom renders. If we do, then we have to be prepared to take the consequences. We will not be given ten of the best on our hands or posteriors for misbehaviour; Jesus is very blunt and tells us that we will not inherit the Kingdom of God.

Sin is rife in our nation and we need to become more aware, making sure it is not in our Christian gatherings. We are deceived into thinking that it is acceptable to 'live together' before marriage, and to be a practising homosexual. It is not. 'Be holy, for I am holy', says God.

The excuse today for allowing sin to govern our lives in some areas, is that if God is love, so everything done in love is permitted. Remember He loves us and hates the sin. He said to Mary Magdalene, who was caught in adultery, **"Go, and <u>sin no more</u>."John 8:11.** (underlining mine)

Fornicators, adulterers, rapists, homosexuals, are all loved and welcomed by God into places of worship where God is respected as supreme, but in order to be a permanent part of a fellowship, we have to truly repent, and 'sin no more'.

1 Corinthians 6:9-11 Do you not know that the unrighteous will not inherit the kingdom of God? Do not be deceived. Neither fornicators, nor idolaters,

nor adulterers, nor homosexuals, nor sodomites, nor thieves, nor covetous, nor drunkards, nor revilers, nor extortioners will inherit the Kingdom of God.

And the last verse tells us: **And such were some of you. But you were washed, but you were sanctified, but you were justified in the name of the Lord Jesus and by the Spirit of our God.**

What is Paul saying in this last verse? When our sins are washed away, we are made holy and are justified in His name. Repentance is called for and His forgiveness is generous. Thus, we should then not want to sin, and be aware when it knocks at our door.

Matthew 24:42-47 "Watch therefore, for you do not know at what hour your Lord is coming. But you know this, that if the master of the house had known at what hour the thief would come he would have watched and not allowed his house to be broken into. Therefore you also be ready, for the Son of Man is coming at an hour when you do not expect Him."

Before we partake of the bread and wine, the precious Body and Blood of Jesus, we must first examine ourselves.

Paul tells us in **1 Corinthians 11:27-32 Therefore**

whoever eats this bread or drinks this cup of the Lord in an unworthy manner will be guilty of the body and blood of the Lord. But let a man examine himself, and so let him eat of that bread and drink of that cup, for he who eats and drinks in an unworthy manner eats and drinks judgement to himself not discerning the Lord's body. For this reason many are weak and sick, among you, and many sleep. For if we would judge ourselves, we would not be judged. But when we are judged, we are chastened by the Lord, that we may not be condemned with the world.

We are unworthy if we have not confessed our sin and repented, so we have no right to receive Holy Communion. To eat His Body and drink His Blood gives us life – spiritual life from spiritual food, so let us stand in awe of His Holiness, have regard and the deepest love and respect for the Man who gave His life for us.

Though it was 'finished' at the cross, He left His Body and Blood with us so as we can eat and drink His life into our spirits.

John 6:63 It is the Spirit who gives life; the flesh profits nothing. The words that I speak to you are spirit and they are life.

Back in 2012 the popular chorus at the time was 'Heal our Nation.' We all longed for God to heal our nation. But even then we were not co-operating with the Lord, and now, eight years on, not only has the nation deteriorated, but it is in dire straights. We have watched God's Laws being eliminated, giving the peoples all that they want so as to appease their appetites.

Since 1950 there have been 24 Ungodly Laws passed in Britain. (You can go to Issacher Ministries for this information.) As Christians we should be ashamed of ourselves. No wonder the world, let alone the nation is in its present state. Where is the Church's authority? Southern Ireland once a country which had also strictly adhered to God's Laws, now permits all they once denounced. Satan has had his way with the Government and its peoples and rejoices in His heydays there, here and throughout the world.

Reader, let us not be neglectful in seeking repentance. The hour is nearly at hand, and Jesus will come like a thief in the night. **1Thessalonians 5:2 For you yourselves know perfectly that the day of the Lord so comes as a thief in the night.**

But let us not be foreboding either; there is hope. **2Peter 3:9 The Lord is not slack concerning His promise, as some**

count slackness, but is long-suffering towards us, not willing that any should perish but that all should come to repentance.

What a patient and merciful God we have. But time is short and we need to put on our skates. Let us seek repentance, and with eager hearts.

We ask Jesus, every time we say His prayer, to forgive us, and in asking thus, we must do a turn around from whatever we are asking Him to forgive us. If we say The Our Father in our church gatherings and know not that we are living in sin, we still must faithfully examine ourselves and ask the Holy Spirit to enlighten us, and when He does, then we must do something about it. If we are made aware that living together with our partners is not acceptable to God, now that we know, we need to arrange to be married or stop living together. But whatever we decide, we must stop co-habiting immediately. Remember that love conquers all things, and when we honour God, He will honour us.

If anyone is a practising homosexual, take heart, God doesn't stop loving you; He sent His Son, Jesus to die for every single soul, without exception. We have been told to welcome all sinners into our midst, but there has to be repentance, a turning away from the sin, the sin which binds us to Satan. **1John 1:9 If we confess our sins, He is faithful and just to forgive us our sins and to cleanse us from all unrighteousness.**

If we steal another's partner, we need to restore them to their rightful place.

If we steal goods from shops, we need to return them, or if we have them no longer, humble ourselves, go back and pay for them.

If we covet something belonging to a friend, we need to let go of the thoughts of 'wanting'.

If we idolise 'things' we need to get our lives into perspective. To idolise anything is to make a god out of it, and our God will not have any gods besides Him. We need to think seriously about the 'things' we posses – what is our attitude towards them. Many could be mentioned, but just to name one - the smart phone. Where are we focused in our church services, our prayer groups and our private prayer times? We need to ask God to search our hearts on this. There is a time and place for everything, and Satan's tactic is to have us distracted, but not in a recognisable or transparent way.

Psalm 139: 3-4 Search me, O God, and know my heart. Try me, and know my anxieties; and see if there is any wicked way in me, and lead me in the way everlasting.

It is a wickedness to idolise anything; let us not play this down. **Exodus 20:3-5 "You shall have no other gods before Me. You shall not make for yourself any carved image, or any likeness of anything that is in heaven above or that is in the earth beneath, or that is in the water under the earth; you shall not bow down to them nor serve them. For I, the Lord your God, am a jealous God, visiting the iniquity of the fathers on the children to the third and fourth generations of those who hate Me; but showing mercy to thousands to those who love Me and keep My commandments."**

Then if we take a look at **Deuteronomy 30: 9-10 we read: The Lord your God will make you abound in all the work of your hand, in the fruit of your body, in the increase of your livestock, and in the produce of your land for good. For the Lord will again rejoice over you for good as He rejoiced over your fathers. If you obey the voice of the Lord your God, to keep His commandments and His statutes which are written in the Book of the Law, and if you turn to the Lord your God with all your heart and with all you soul.**

Deuteronomy 30 is under the title in the NKJV 'The Blessing of Returning to God.' It is worth reading.

One might think that because the above is in the Old Testament, it does do not apply in the 21st century; after all, everything today, even the people, are different from all those years ago. Be not deceived, God's commandments are as relevant today as they were then. Many laws that we read about in the Old Testament were there for the Jews at the time, but when Jesus came these were done away with; He atoned for our sins. However, the Ten Commandments still remain and must be adhered to. Remember God does not change, not like man, who is fickle and changes his colours like a chameleon.

There are many verses with regard God not changing, **Hebrews 13:8** being one of the most popular. **Jesus Christ is the same yesterday, today and forever;** and one that gives total assurity, **Isaiah 40:8 The grass withers, the flower fades, but the word of our God will stand forever.**

Psalm 51:1-19 is a prayer of repentance for David. We can use it for our own repentant prayer if we find we do not have suitable words ourselves. Many of the Psalms can be prayed as our own prayers. The whole of Psalm 51 needs to be read/prayed, and indeed one is able to feel David's regret and sorrow for his sin. To quote: **verse 17: The sacrifices of God are a broken spirit, a broken and contrite heart – these O God, you will not despise.**

God does not despise sincerity and true sorrow, and to think that there are angels in heaven that rejoice over the repentance of one sinner.

Luke 15:7 "I say to you that likewise there will be more joy in heaven over one sinner who repents than over ninety-nine just persons who need no repentance."

Doesn't that make you want to clap your hands!

And let us remember with gratitude that: **There is now no condemnation to those who are in Christ Jesus, who do not walk according to the flesh, but according to the Spirit. Romans 8:1.** Amen.

THAT ONE DAY A WEEK

How far have we walked since our first encounter with the Lord Jesus? Do we ever ask ourselves - are we still moving forward, going backward, or, have we come to a standstill?

The Sabbath day was a gift to us from God, and it is on this special day we could take the above questions, look at them one by one and see what answer we arrive at. Whatever the answer, it's okay, because God is for us, not against us, and as long as we bother to take time out to check ourselves we are fine.

God made the world in six days and on the seventh day He rested. He commanded us to do the same on the seventh, thereby giving us time to re-charge our batteries, ready and rested for the onslaught of another week. It is also a time when we are to praise and worship Him.

How many of us acknowledge this special day of rest? How many of us do not go Sunday shopping? This was another downfall of this once Christian nation. We turned our backs on God - again.

God doesn't change; He is the same yesterday, today and forever, as we can read many times through Scripture. His

Commandments are still relevant today and yet they are discarded, seemingly as being out-dated and irrelevant. We need to wake up, we need to stay awake, we need to become God pleasers and not man pleasers, we need to honour the Sabbath as we are commanded to do, and in doing so we honour Him.

Exodus 20:8-11. Remember the Sabbath day and keep it holy.

In **Luke 23:55-56** we read that after Jesus was buried in the tomb, **women who had come with Him from Galilee followed after, and they observed the tomb and how His body was laid. Then they returned and prepared spices and fragrant oils. <u>And they rested on the Sabbath according to the commandment.</u>** (underlining mine)

Take note this was <u>after</u> the death of Jesus, so if He had withdrawn this commandment, would they not have known?

Why would God list the Ten Commandments in the first place and then decide because they did not please man, remove one, some, or perhaps all of them?

Hebrews 4:9 There remains therefore a rest for the people of God. For He who entered His rest has Himself

also ceased from His works as God did from His. To understand it fully, it would be worthwhile reading the chapter from the beginning down to verse 10. It comes under the title 'The Promise of Rest.'

We are constantly running around in square circles, fingers tapping relentlessly on mobiles and computers. We make our lives frantic by our meanderings; we need to take time out and rest awhile; put all the gadgets away and focus on Him. But no, we insist we do not have the time, like the Israelites, indulging in other activities, being stiff necked, wanting to please ourselves; God is pushed out - see you later – what ever that means and - 'I'm too busy.' Is it much to ask for that one day a week? We should welcome the opportunity to switch off, not just our gadgets, but our swirling minds, to take time even to 'smell the roses' on our day of rest. He wants us to enjoy our day off. We also need to learn how to separate our thoughts.

Separating Thoughts

It's good to filter through the tides of thought,
in fact one ought to do it regularly.
For like the sea, whose tides rush in and out,
clearing, sifting, from what's underneath,
discarding, bringing in relief, a cleansing – so
we too, should sift our thoughts each day,
throw those away that steal our peace,
find that niche on the gentle shores of life,
trusting energies that perhaps we fear.
Tide and time await no man, so as we sift
through our thought zone and learn to separate
each thought one from another, we will discover
how to live a fuller life, achieving, and in our God believing.

*****

"My kingdom is not of this world" were the words of Jesus in **John 18:36.** If this is so, nor is it ours. We are in transit, but we need to follow the correct path else we will stray and end up in a lost eternity. No Christian wants or desires that, but though God is merciful, He is also just and fair. It is easy to attend church on Sundays, listen to the Word, sing hymns and delight ourselves in worship. Hopefully we delight Him more than ourselves.

He demands a 'holy people'. One may ask, what is 'holy'? It is a coming out of the world, sacrificing our Sundays, respecting His commands, walking in righteousness. If we stand back and take a look at ourselves, would we be shocked? Many of us are not much different from those who do not believe; countless shop on Sundays, watch bad television, and misuse the mobile phone. However, <u>would</u> we be shocked at our behaviour?

Try standing for a few minutes without the mobile amongst a crowd - listen to the atmosphere - what is happening? Surely we must recognise that something isn't right? However, we need to put ourselves in order before we can put others on the straight and narrow. Take out the plank first!

We are not perfect human beings, all being flawed with Adam's sin, but because God sent Jesus to deal with our flawed humanness, we are set free and in this freedom we can exercise our love, our commitment to a flawless God. Let us recognise the world for what it is and all it has to offer under the guise of Satan. Let us not be afraid of being different.

As **2 Timothy 7** says, **For God has not given us a spirit of fear, but of power and of love and of a sound mind.**

Thus with a spirit of bravery, of power, of love and in total sanity, we must come out from among them and be separate. This is not always easy. We don't want to feel and look different from those with whom we work, socialise and live. Of course, we all have choices, and when we choose God's way, it is the right way and one we would never regret.

We have to understand what is meant by coming out from amongst them and being separate. We must not partake of anything that is not in agreement with the Lord. To be able to do this, we have to take time out and pray and ask for wisdom, which we know from **James 1:2-7** how to obtain this valuable and necessary asset.

We need to pray daily for the blessing of wisdom. Not to be wise in our own eyes, but having the eyes of God in our daily lives. Even down to the shopping list! The benefits of God's wisdom outweigh everything.

Proverbs 3:7 tells us not to be wise in our own eyes. **Do not be wise in your own eyes; fear the Lord and depart from evil. It will be health to your flesh, and strength to your bones.**

It would be good to read the whole of the Proverb, as it spells out such wisdom.

Shopping on Sundays, though it has become quite a natural thing to do, is really at variance with God. When He commands us to keep the Sabbath holy, though the government gave the go ahead for Sunday trading, Christians had the right to object by just not shopping. We could have voted with our feet and still can do.

But, we came up with excuses, one being how convenient it was, it suited our circumstances. <u>We fitted in with the world</u>. And as **Timothy** says in **Chapter 6:7 We brought nothing into this world, and it is certain that we can carry nothing out. And having food and clothing, with these we shall be content.**

There were those who objected, and I am sure there are many who still hold fast to the no shopping on Sunday policy, but one fears that they are in the minority. When we read about the Israelites in **Exodus 35:16**, let us think about their situation, and the regulations that were put down for them. We do not have to adhere to all the articles of the tabernacle and offerings that they were called to make. **<u>However, we are called to set the Sabbath day aside just for God</u>.**

Yes, we live in different days, we are different people, living in the 21st century, but we must always keep in mind that God does not change, nor do His Commandments. We are let off pretty lightly in comparison to the Israelites, and why – because of Jesus, and we have Him to thank for being the final offering on the alter.

Shall we think about shopping on Sunday? How would we fare if we didn't go to the shops?

Let us look again at the Israelites when they 'murmured' (complained) against Moses and Aaron. **Exodus 16:2.** Then in **verse 4 .....** The Lord said to Moses, **"Behold, I will rain bread from heaven for you. And the people shall go out and gather a certain quota every day, that I may test them, whether they will walk in My law or not."**

And **verse 5 ....** **"And it shall be on the sixth day that they shall prepare what they bring in, and it shall be twice as much as they gather daily."**

They then had quail in the evenings. However it was a <u>daily</u> 'shopping' for them, they were not to take more than was needed – except on the day before the Sabbath, they were to collect twice as much, so as they didn't need to go 'shopping' on the Sabbath. Those who disobeyed found that their supplies went rotten. Suggest to read the whole of **Exodus 16.**

Paul tells us in **Phillipians 4:9 that ... my God will supply all our needs, according to His riches in glory by Christ Jesus.** Let us take Him at His word.

Are we afraid by not shopping on Sunday we will have to go without, or we won't have enough? There are times that it is good to go without the usual 'must haves'. It can be a way of fasting as well, which feeds us spiritually. There are the other six days when we can shop to ensure we have enough for meals on Sunday. We need to acknowledge this obvious fact and not join the crowds of Sunday shoppers.

God is not a spoil sport. He has blessed us with the day of rest to be able to enjoy it. We can go out walking, and when in the calm we can listen and hear. There are always whispers in the air, in the quietness, in the wind or gentle breeze – **'in the still small voice'. 1Kings 19:11.**

Whispers in the Wind

Listening doesn't have to be an art, for if the heart is open, it hears the whispers of a breeze, the flowers, grass and trees – all say something special.

There are secrets in the wind and at times the din of life is too loud to hear what it is saying.

We need to take time out in the business of life to listen.

It is so easy to close out the sound of silence that is ours to take,

afraid to be alone with thoughts and pain and grief.

But know the world and all it has to offer in materialism

can be a daily thief, robbing us of secrets whispered in the wind.

We need a quiet niche to put our troubled souls away, even

if for just a moment in a day.

We need a soothing peace, a hide away,

We need to hear the whispers in the wind.

Let us not forsake the God who created man in His own image, who sent His Son, Jesus, to atone for our wrong doings. Let us show our love for Him, our appreciation, through obedience. Let us be grateful that we were given a day where we are able to gather our thoughts, put the world aside, and simply 'be'.

Exodus 20:8-11 "Remember the Sabbath day, to keep it holy. Six days you shall labour and do your work but the seventh day is the Sabbath of the Lord your God: in it you shall not do any work……".

Luke 4:16 – Jesus kept the Sabbath by going into the synagogue and stood up to read.

Colossians 2:16 – Paul teaches not to let others condemn us for keeping the Sabbath.

Let us keep that one day a week just for Him.

*****

THERE IS ONLY ONE TRUTH

I am the Way, the Truth and the Life – words of Jesus, words that do not need to be analysed, words that just are, words that tell us – the Truth - if we recognise and believe that Jesus is Who He says He is.

Why then is it necessary to write about it, one might ask. Because there are so many untruths in today's world, it is possible Christians need another wake up call, so as to recognise Satan's lies which He covers over with surreptitious ardour. There are no flies on him.

There is so much deceit in life, we need to focus on that which we know is the Truth. Perhaps we need reminding, given that there are so many distractions which fool us into believing the falsehoods that appear to be genuine, are actually erroneous lies. We are, at times, quite gullible, yes, even Christians can live under a certain amount of gullibility; maybe we are in the world too much and do not realise it. Maybe we need a little shaking!

In John 18:37-38 we read when Jesus was arrested and taken before Pilate. who asked, **"Are you a king then?" Jesus answered. "You say rightly that I am a king. For this cause I was born, and for this cause I have come into the**

world, that I should bear witness to the Truth. <u>Everyone who is of the Truth hears my voice</u>. Pilate said to Him, "What is Truth." And when he had said this he went out again to the Jews, and said to them. "I find no fault in Him at all."** (underlining mine) Did Pilate believe Him? Perhaps he did, maybe he did recognise the Truth, but was afraid.

Do we hear His voice today? Are we listening? Are we staying awake? Are we afraid? These are questions we need to ask ourselves seriously. The distractions around belie us, which is a trick in Satan's trade. It appears that though we believe, and have faith, we listen more to him and all his handouts, extending credence to his philosophies and false values. Why is this? If Jesus is Who He says He is, 'The Truth', why do we follow untruths in the world? Feasibly the offerings in the world are fun, one believes they are innocent, and hey, let's enjoy what we can whilst we can! But we know that Satan is the Father of lies.

Luke 12:15-21 covers this attitude. **"…Teacher tell my brother to divide the inheritance with me." But he said to him, "Man, who made me a judge or an arbitrator over you?" And he said to them, "Take heed and beware of covetousness, for one's life does not consist in the abundance of the things he possesses."** Then He spoke a parable to them, saying. **"The ground of a certain rich man yielded plentifully. And he thought within himself, saying. 'What shall I do since I have no room to store my crops?' So he said, 'I will do this: I will pull down my barns and build greater, and there I will store all my crops and my goods. And I will say to my soul. "Soul, you have many goods laid up for years; take your ease; eat, drink and be merry"' But God said to him 'You fool! This night your soul will be required of you; then whose will those things be which you have provided?' "So is he who who lays up treasure for himself, and is not rich towards God."**

Does that speak to us? Do we allow it to? Are we listening? The world is a clatter and a clutter with so much paraphernalia, at times, or most of the time, we do not know whether we are coming or going. We have to do neither. **Turn not to the left or to the right. Remove your foot from evil. Proverbs 4:27.**

It would be of value to read the whole of Proverbs 4, which is titled 'Security in Wisdom'.

We need to come to a place where we are able to be still physically, mentally, emotionally and spiritually. Why? Because if we don't we won't be ready when Jesus comes again. Of course He wants us to enjoy many of the honest enjoyable things in the world, but these need to be limited. We have all heard of 'fake news' and this is nothing new. If we look in **Matthew 28:11-15 Now while they were going, behold some of guards came into the city and reported to the chief priests all the things that had happened. When they had assembled with the elders and taken counsel, they gave a large sum of money to the soldiers, saying, "Tell them, 'His disciples came at night and stole Him away while we slept.' "And if this comes to the governor's ears, we will appease him and make you secure." So they took the money and did as they were instructed, <u>and this saying is commonly reported among the Jews until this day</u>.** (It is always a good idea to read the proceeding verses so as to have the story line in context.) (underlining mine)

Yes, 'even to this day' the year 2021; if ever there was fake news this has to be the best, and the reason, no doubt, that so many Jews and countless people in general, are still in the dark. Many Jews still live within the confines of the Old Testament because of this fake news. An unadulterated tragedy.

As Christians, we must learn to discern that which is false and that which is true. Surely the one and only way to differentiate between them is to focus on Who and what is 'Truth'. Jesus said that He would lead us into all Truth, so let us believe Him. **John 16:13 "However, when He, the Spirit of Truth comes, He will guide you into all Truth; for He will not speak on His own authority, but whatever He hears He will speak; and He will tell you things to come..."**

The world is full of falsity, lulling us into a false sense of security, encouraging us to build our hopes on social media and the rest. **"Come out from among them and be separate." says the Lord. 2 Corinthians 17a.**

What an invitation! Or - is it a demand? For God wants a holy people, and if we are to be what He wants, then we must eagerly obey His calling.

We need to turn our backs on the world and our faces toward the Truth. The internet is Satan's web, and though it has become for the majority, a necessary part of life, we need to be wise as to its use.

Let us be like the man in **Luke 6:48** who built his house on the rock, and not like the other one who built his on sand. This parable of Jesus is telling us to build our lives on Him, not on the world. The world doesn't have a foundation, whereas Jesus is our foundation. So let us build on the rock as Jesus suggests. **"Whoever comes to me, and hears my sayings and does them, I will show you whom he is like.**

He is like a man building a house, who dug deep and laid the foundation on the rock. And when the flood arose, the stream beat vehemently against that house, and could not shake it, for it was founded on the rock. But he who heard and did nothing is like a man who built a house on the earth without a foundation, against which the stream beat vehemently, and immediately it fell. And the ruin of that house was great."

This is excellent and wise advice and we have a choice whether to go along with it or not. We will always have a free will, but once we give our lives over to the Lord, then He expects obedience. He is our Father, and fathers discipline their children – why? - because they love them and want their happiness.

Truth is spoken of in the Old Testament. Let us look at **1Kings 17:24 Then the woman said to Elijah, "Now by this I know that you are a man of God, and that the word of the Lord in your mouth is the <u>Truth</u>".** (underlining mine)

Her son had died and she blamed Elijah for his death, but he took him and brought him back to life – thus her faith was restored, believing that he <u>was</u> a man of <u>Truth</u>. For her, and Elijah, <u>God was Truth</u>.

Proverbs give many words of wisdom, and **Chapter 12:22** tells us that: **Lying lips are an abomination to the Lord, but those who deal truthfully are His delight.**

And last, but no means least, there is **Psalm 145:18 The Lord is near to all who call on, to all who call on Him in Truth.**

There are, as we know, many passages on Truth in the New Testament as well, but again just to mention a few.

John 8:31-32 Then Jesus said to those Jews who believed Him, "If you abide in my word, you are my disciples indeed. And you shall know the Truth, and the Truth shall make you free." Jesus was speaking of Himself as being the Truth, and we are made free if we live in Him and experience what this freedom does in us and for us.

1Corinthians 13: ... talking of love, Paul says in **verse 6 – it does not rejoice in iniquity but rejoices in the Truth.**

Psalm 25:5 Lead me in your Truth and teach me, for you are the God of my salvation; on you I wait all the day.

And finally, though not the last of many more is **John 4:23-24 "But the hour is coming, and now is, when the true worshippers will worship the Father in Spirit and Truth, for the Father is seeking such to worship Him. God is a Spirit, and those who worship Him must worship in Spirit and Truth."**

Jesus says that He requires Truth in our inmost beings. **Psalm 51:6 Behold you desire Truth in the inward parts, and in the hidden part you will make me to know wisdom.** And we know, as believers, what that means. When we have the courage to look deep into our inmost selves, and ask God to search out our hearts, then we are able to discern the truths and untruths in the world – those which are fake and those which are true.

Let us be true to ourselves, root out that which is untrue and live in Truth – for - There is Only One Truth – Jesus Christ, the Son of the Living God.

HE SUPPLIES ALL OUR NEEDS

We all have to face up to making decisions, big and small, and more often than not we need to consult our heavenly Father on the most important issues. However, what about the seemingly, insignificant ones, every day matters such as shopping? Oh! Why would He be interested in shopping? What do you mean? - for food, clothes, furniture and every sort of thing we might buy during our shopping sprees?

Believe it or not, our heavenly Father is extremely interested, and not only in what we purchase, but whom we meet, with whom we converse, our friendships and much more. Let us ask ourselves who supplies all these necessities? **And my God shall supply all your needs according to His riches in glory by Christ Jesus. Phillipians 4:19.** (underlining mine)

Why did Paul write this? If we read the verses beforehand, it tells us that the churches were not sharing with him, but Epaphroditus was. If we cannot obtain what we need through one source, God supplies another. Or, perhaps we will have to go without sometimes – and there is always a reason for this, which is wise to think on.

Ecclesiastes 3 tell us that there is a purpose for <u>everything</u> under the sun!

And **Psalm 57:2 I will cry out to God Most High, To God who performs all things for me.**

In other words - <u>Who fulfils His purposes for me</u>.

We might think it silly to ask Him whether we should buy this or that, or cook rice or potatoes for lunch; after all we are sensible adults and it would be somewhat ridiculous having to consult Him on everything to do with our needs.

Look at this way. He is the supplier of all our needs, and hopefully we give Him thanks for them. (not be like nine of the ten lepers who never returned to give thanks – **Luke 17:11-19**) - why not chat about them with Him beforehand as well? We don't have to get down on our hands and knees, just talk to Him as we go about our daily lives. It's also fun!

Having daily, ordinary conversations with our beloved Lord is a strengthening of faith, and forms a unique and wonderful <u>friendship</u> with the Holy Spirit, who Jesus promised would always be with us. It probably would be easier, one might think, not to have anyone around, but circumstances shouldn't deter us from forming a friendship with our Saviour. Quiet chats with Him in our thoughts is a wonderful way in which to converse. He knows and hears our thoughts, which is something the devil cannot do, so it can be a secret and sacred place of retreat for just the two of you.

Psalm 139:2 You know my sitting down and my rising up, You understand <u>my thought</u> afar off. (underlining mine)

And 7-10 Where can I go from your Spirit? Or where can I flee from your presence? If I ascend into heaven, you are there. If I make my bed in hell, behold, you are there. If I take the wings of the morning, and dwell in the uttermost part of the sea, even there your hand shall lead me, and your right hand shall hold me.

The whole Psalm makes for a wonderful read.

When Elijah, the prophet, was alone at the Brook Cherith, he didn't even have to ask for his needs to be met – they came to him automatically by the hand of God. No doubt after his travels, he was not only tired, but very hungry, so asked the widow for some bread. She was reluctant to give her last piece, as it was for her and her son, but she adhered to his request, and afterwards God kept her supply going as was needed. **1Kings17:8-16.**

So, too, He gives us what we need at times without us asking. But again, let us always remember to thank Him.

Quite often we think we want something, but having bought it, after a while realise we don't really care for it.

To quote C. S. Lewis - 'The desire is always in the wanting and not in the having.' We need to learn to be content with what we have and not crave for things that are not really necessities. Obviously, we must be discerning over all our 'must haves', 'wants' and 'needs'. God does often bless us with 'wants', and then it is up to us to keep things in perspective.

Life's journey is fascinating, what with all the manageable and seemingly unmanageable learning curves we face daily. It helps to have a healthy attitude. God does give us the desires of our heart, but always only the things which are of His heart as well. Though there are times, unfortunately, because we have been so demanding, that when He does give us what we want, it has proven to be detrimental!

<u>Delight yourself in the Lord</u>, and He shall give you the desires of your heart. Psalm 37:4. (underling mine)

He understands our weaknesses, our humanity, with so many decisions we find ourselves having to make. But if we consult Him, He is ever faithful to advise us. We must honour Him, obey Him, walk with Him in honesty; do as best as we are able, and He promises that He will be always with us – even until the end of time. ... **"and lo, I am with you always, even to the end of the age." Amen." Matthew 28:20b.**

Ecclesiastes 3 tells us that that there is a season for everything. It makes for an interesting read.

It is quite extraordinary knowing that there are many, many people in this country who do not have enough to eat, and rely on hand-outs and food-banks. In a society where millions of pounds are spent on what are thought to be important and necessary for the survival of us all, God must agonise over the terrible waste. Yes, He does supply all our needs according to His riches in glory, but there has to be a cut of point surely.

The nation has cast aside most of, if not all, God's laws. He is demeaned, cursed and blamed for so much that is wrong. Does man not have any responsibility? God is decried, even though to many He doesn't even exist! He is blamed for the bad things and man is praised for the good! There is something not right here.

If God is not honoured, than how can we expect Him to honour us? We only have to take a look at the Israelites whilst in the wilderness with Moses. Their turning away from worshipping the One True God, making a moulded calf to worship instead; complaining all the time; not walking in step with the law. All this disobedience led them to wander for 40 years, and then not the original people, but their descendants, were permitted into the promised land. And we expect God to supply all our needs when we live in disobedience ourselves, make 'golden calves' and dis-honour Him. He honours only those who honour Him.

In **1 Samuel 2:22-36** we are told of the 'Prophecy Against Eli's Household.' This should still speak to us today, for God does not change and He will not be mocked. - **for those who honour me I will honour, and those who despise me shall be lightly esteemed.**

It is recommended to read it all.

He will always supply all our needs, according to His riches in glory, but let us remember to honour and obey His everlasting laws in order for Him to do just that.

There are many places in Scripture reassuring its readers of God's love, and of the consequences of our refusal to walk in His ways. We cannot, and should not, as Christians, expect to have our needs met, if we aren't on line with Him. We walk a narrow and straight path, and as David says in **Psalm 23 '...I shall not want.'** and in **Psalm 25** as he lifted up his soul he said, **2 O my God, I trust in you...** and 4-5 **'Show me Your ways, O Lord, teach me Your paths. Lead me in Your truth and teach me, for you are the God of my salvation. On You I wait all the day.'**

Many of the Psalms can be said as prayers for others as well as ourselves. 'Show them/her/him your ways.... Teach them/her/him your paths... Turn yourself to them/her/him and have mercy on them/her/him, for they/she/he are/is desolate and afflicted. The troubles of their/his/her heart/s have enlarged.

It is an honour to use David's prayers privately for one's self but particularly for others, when we cannot find the words ourselves. Never be hesitant in doing this. David was a man after God's own heart, and a man of deep prayer. We can be the same no matter who we are, remembering that **... God looks at the heart. Samuel 17:7.**

And in **Acts 13:32** Paul preaching in a synagogue with regard Israel at the time of King Saul, when they had removed him from kingship, David was raised up as king, saying what God had said, **"I have found David the son of Jesse, a man after my own heart, who will do all my will."**

There is nothing to stop us from being people after God's own heart; nothing except a refusal to be so. We are not asked to be kings or queens, we are not asked to be great leaders; we are simply asked to be ourselves; to be the people God made us to be; to live as best we can in honesty and truth. We are not perfect and will not be until we go to be with Him; we will always make mistakes, take wrong turns, say wrong things, think wrong thoughts, but as long as we repent daily and walk with Him, have no doubt **He will always supply all our needs, according to His riches in glory. Phillipians 4:19.**

What about the rich? Does God supply all their needs? It may seem so, but it is the world that looks after the rich who do not honour God. They have all that they want and need at any time. Is that fair especially when many of God's faithful appear to be on the 'bread line'? We are told that the rich who do not know God, will not enter the kingdom of heaven.

We have only to read **Luke 16:19-31** which relates the story of the rich man and Lazarus. This is quite an eye opener.

There are, of course, many wealthy people who are extremely generous to the poor, and believe in Christ. But 'believe' is the password. No matter how much an unbeliever gives to the less well off, if he does not believe in God, than he is a lost soul.

Let us take a look at **Matthew 19:16-24** where Jesus counsels the rich young ruler as to his question **'what good thing shall I do that I may have eternal life?'**, listing all the laws he has kept since a youth.

But Jesus said to him, **"If you want to be perfect, go, sell what you have and give to the poor, and you will have treasure in heaven, and come, follow me." But when the young man heard that saying, he went away sorrowful, for he had great possessions.**

Nevertheless, we have a compassionate and understanding God, always having mercy on whom He will have mercy, and when we are ready to give our lives to Him we will know this. There are Christians who are endowed with riches and they use them to aid those who need it, not holding back from what they have been commissioned to do. He is also a forgiving God, as we know from the 'good thief' crucified next to Him, as he acknowledged Him as the Son of God. All his past wrongs were forgiven in an instant, as Jesus saw his heart of sorrow and repentance, and promised that he would be in paradise with Him. **Luke 23:39-43.**

In the 21st century in our land, beggars are still on our streets; homeless people shelter under bridges and in alley ways, and we pass them without a word, perhaps hanging our heads, pretending not to notice them. God will supply their needs through us if we are willing and ready to give. There might be fake beggars, but who are we to judge; let us give without counting the cost, for God loves a cheerful giver. **2 Corinthians 6-11.**

There is a story of a young man buying a sandwich and giving it to a beggar on the street. Noticing the disappointment on the beggar's face, the man realised he really wanted a beer! He went back to the shop, bought two cans and on giving him one, then sat down with him, in his city suit, and they both drank and chatted for a while. Was that not Christ Himself in both forms – the beggar and the giver? For every kind deed we do for someone we do for Christ. In this way He supplies all our needs according to His riches in glory.

We only only have to read about St. Francis, who apparently had a loathing for lepers, and one day whilst out riding on his horse, came across one. He dismounted, and though filled with utter disgust, for some reason kissed him. Looking back after the incident, he realised it had been Jesus. He wrote in his testimony that whilst he was in sin, lepers repulsed him, but when he met Christ in one, he learnt pity and compassion. Whether this be myth or not is really neither here nor there, it is a fine example of how needs are met spiritually.

Helen Keller (1880-1968) though blind, deaf and mute had her needs met through a faithful Irish woman, Anne Sullivan. She taught her to see through touch, to hear through touch and to speak through touch. God never deserted them and they were faithful to Him.

Man is so needful is so many areas. Mental, physical, emotional, social and spiritual, and all these can be met by our Saviour.

Psalm 20:7-8 Some trust in chariots, and some in horses, but we will remember the name of the Lord our God. They have bowed down and fallen, but we have risen and stand upright.

RIGHTEOUSNESS AND SELF RIGHTEOUSNESS

Righteous. What does it mean? Am I righteous? Are you righteous? If not, should we be righteous? If so why and what makes us thus?

We have to differentiate between being righteous and **self**-righteous. There is a vast difference between the meaning, and by just the one that one word – **self**.

We can all suffer from **self**-righteousness. To say 'suffer', is what **self**-righteous people do – they 'suffer', and are insufferable to themselves and others.

To suffer as a **self**-righteous person is not in the way that one usually thinks of when it comes to suffering. Jesus suffered on the cross, He suffered from thirst, He suffered extreme pain, pain which is unexplainable, pain from our sins; He was whipped and scourged, tormented beyond belief, sneered at, spat at, humiliated and betrayed.

Being **self**-righteous does not cause any of the above sufferings; **Self**-righteous people are 'know alls', thinking that they are right in everything and their beliefs will not be challenged. 'I'm right and that's that!' Have you been, or are you like that? Maybe you know someone who is.

There are of course many areas in our lives where we are right, but to the unbeliever it might possibly come across as being **self-** righteous – we believe that there is a God, and that He sent His Son Jesus to die for the world. But for that to come across as seeming **self**-righteous, can only drive people away, not draw them toward the Truth we wish to convey. So one must have wisdom and pray for sensitivity, at the same time holding on to what are fundamental truths.

Psalm 139:23-24 Search me, O God, and know my heart; try me, and know my anxieties; and see if there is any wicked way in me, and lead me in the way everlasting.

If we allow God to do just that, then we will gradually learn to let go of our **self**-righteous attitudes and accept that to be righteous is not of ourselves, but is ours <u>through</u> Jesus. And if we hunger and thirst for it, we shall be filled, and ours is the kingdom of heaven – as stated in **Matthew 5:6 and 10, (part of the Beatitudes) "Blessed are those who hunger and thirst for righteousness, for they shall be <u>satisfied</u>. (underlining mine) Blessed are those who are persecuted for righteousness sake, for theirs is the kingdom of heaven."**

Having learnt the difference, the word 'satisfied' becomes real. Now we feel satisfied that we are not being, or feeling, **self**-righteous, but we <u>know that we are made righteous through Jesus; it is His righteousness living inside of us</u>. That is some revelation! The feeling (which is one of indignation) of **self**-righteousness is no longer within us, just righteousness with God.

Christians are objects of hostility, or are persecuted; they are oft times 'put down'; are told that they are weird; they are ridiculed, ignored and laughed at for their belief. To argue with the opposition is always pointless; to discuss differences in a mature manner can prove to have far reaching results. Hostility walks hand in hand with Christianity, but it can make us stronger if we face up to it wisely.

We need to be humble enough to remain teachable and open minded to other's views and beliefs. The fact that we believe in Christ, however, is not being **self**-righteous, it is a right belief in God's promise - **that if you confess with your mouth the Lord Jesus and believe in your heart that God raised Him from the dead, you will be saved. Romans 10:9-10.** And it is only when we are born again of the spirit* can we believe this and have peace in our hearts. But, I repeat, this is not being **self**-righteous. We are then in right standing with

God. He sees us as obedient sons of God.

*To be 'born again of the spirit' is important for eternal life. If we look at **John's Gospel 3:3 Jesus answered and said to him, "Most assuredly, I say to you, unless one is born again, he cannot see the kingdom of God."**

Verses 1-21 explains about God's people being born again. The term 'born again' causes animosity at times with those who do not understand its meaning. Understandably, as one has to be 'born again' in order to have understanding of spiritual things!

As Christians we are very diverse, and diversity makes for an interesting life. We have all been created in God's image, but we are created with assorted personalities, different characters, but as born again believers, we all believe in the one God and His Son, Jesus.

We pray and worship variously, because we are individuals. You might wash and dry the dishes differently from members of your family or your spouse. You might fill the kettle to the brim in order to make a cup of tea, whereas someone else puts in just enough water for one cup of tea. You might shower or bath in the mornings, others do so at night. Do we think the other is wrong in doing it their way?

Some folk do! Does it matter? It really is so unimportant that it doesn't require a mention at all. I allude to it merely to point out a simple fact, with simple examples of our human diversity.

It is known that thousands of Christians have stopped attending church because of the way services are presented, or because of now differing beliefs, in that the leaders and some of the congregations are compromising their faith by being 'man pleasers', rather than God pleasers.

Jeremiah 17:5 has something to say on this. **Thus says the Lord; "cursed is the man that trusts in man, and makes flesh his arm, and whose heart departs from the Lord."**

And again, in **Acts 5:28** when the apostles were imprisoned for speaking about Jesus, having been told not to do so by those in authority "**…..Did we not strictly command you not to teach in this name?"**

And in verse 29 … But Peter and the other apostles answered and said: "We ought to obey God rather than men."

Are they judging, criticising, or being self-righteous or righteous, by not attending church? Hopefully the reason for not attending would be righteous – being in **right standing**

with God - because we know, through the promptings of the Holy Spirit that the church's representation isn't what it should be - in God's eyes. Not what we think it should be, or would like it to be, but that it is not honouring to our Creator. **John 12:26 "If anyone serves me, let him follow me; and where I am, there my servant will be also. If anyone serves me, him My Father will honour."**

Now, we mustn't have the 'holier than thou' attitude – to be this would be extremely **self**-righteous. Again, this is where we ask God to: **Search me O God, and know my heart, and see if there is any wicked way in me, and lead me in the way everlasting. Psalm 139:23-24.** If we often read this extraordinary and wonderful Psalm, it will help us come to grips with our very being, and be made to realise just who we are in Christ.

Isaiah 55:8-9 "For My thoughts are not your thoughts, nor are your ways my ways," says the Lord. "For as the heavens are higher than the earth, so are my ways higher than your ways, and my thoughts than your thoughts."

Doesn't this reading also help to keep life in perspective? We have a great and Holy God; we are mere mortals, like ants rushing hither and thither, this way and that, and yet He loves us mightily, and simply asks us to conduct our lives in such a way that we glorify Him. We must **'come out and be separate'** **2 Corinthians 6:17**; we not only have to, but we should <u>want</u> to be separate from those who do not, and do not care to live His way.

It is very easy to have a **self**-righteous attitude. We might boast that we do not watch certain television programmes, are not on Face book or do not use particular 'apps'. We have to remember that we all have choices and if some choose to watch unhealthy programmes or indulge in Face book, that is their choice. To say that we don't, and they shouldn't, with a **self**-righteous attitude, is just that, **self**-righteousness. It's learning to let go of 'I'm better than they', to discern that we are not <u>better</u> than they, but <u>better off.</u> Wouldn't that be kinder? And the truth!

Our attitudes boil down to knowing where we are in Christ. As human beings we are born into sin, but that sin is removed by Jesus having shed His precious blood for us, with us acknowledging this, repenting of our sins and asking Jesus to live within us. However, this doesn't make us perfect human beings; we will only become perfect when we rise from the dead at the second coming of Jesus. We are still sinners, therefore we are advised to confess our sins to one another, and pray for one another.

James 5:16 tells us to: **Confess your trespasses to one another, and pray one for another, that you maybe healed. The effective, fervent prayer of a <u>righteous</u> man avails much.** (underlining mine)

Life suddenly doesn't lose all its problems, but my goodness, we can hand them all over to the One who has promised that He will never leave us nor forsake us. **Hebrews 13:5-6. for He has said, "I will never leave you nor forsake you."**

These promises are in various books of the Bible, Old and New Testaments, and it is worth searching for them. To do this can be exciting, and on locating them you will feel more and more encouraged, as along the way you will find yourself reading other verses, not relevant to what you were looking for, but speak to you nevertheless.

Jane, in Charlotte Bronte's novel, Jane Eyre, gives a fine example of righteousness, when as a child, she stands up to her aunt. One may think of Jane as being disrespectful, and indeed as a child she was, and should not have spoken to her aunt in the manner that she did. But, Jane was bullied and disrespected by her aunt, and felt cheated, unloved, in fact hated, by her and the rest of the family. She was finally driven to an outrageous outburst. Even as a ten year old child she was in the right and her aunt in the wrong, and though it is not given that youngsters voice their disapproval, especially in what Jane said, her anger, her hurt, her indignant attitude, surely, was **righteous**.

I quote from the novel, parts of Chapter 4.

I had regained my normal health, but no new allusion was made to the subject over which I brooded. Mrs Reed surveyed me at times with a severe eye, but seldom addressed me; since my illness she had drawn a more marked line of separation than ever between me and her own children, appointing me a small closet to sleep in by myself, condemning me to take my meals alone, and pass all my time in the nursery, while my cousins were constantly in the drawing-room....

Eliza and Georgiana, evidently acting according to orders, spoke to me as little as possible; John thrust his tongue in his cheek whenever he saw me, and once attempted chastisement; but as I instantly turned against him, roused by the same sentiment of deep ire and desperate revolt which had stirred my corruption before, he thought it better to desist, and ran from me, uttering execrations, and vowing I had burst his nose. I had, indeed, levelled at that prominent feature as hard a blow as my knuckles could inflict; and when I saw that either that or my look daunted him I had the greatest inclination to follow up my advantage to purpose, but he was already with his mamma.

I heard him in a blubbering tone commence the tale of how 'that nasty Jane Eyre' had flown at him like a mad cat; he was stopped rather harshly --

'Don't talk to me about her, John; I told you not to go near her: she is not worthy of notice. I do not choose that either you or your sister should associate with her.'

Here, leaning over the banister, I cried out suddenly, and without at all deliberation on my words –

'They are not fit to associate with me.'

Mrs Reed was rather a stout woman; but on hearing this strange and audacious declaration, she ran nimbly up the stair, swept me like a whirlwind into the nursery, and crushing me down on the edge of my crib, dared me in an emphatic voice to rise from that place, or utter one syllable, during the remainder of the day.

The following, uttered by Jane Eyre, has to be her righteous hurt and anger.

'What would Uncle Reed say to you, if he were alive?' was my scarcely voluntary demand. I say scarcely voluntary, for it seemed as if my tongue pronounced words without my will consenting to their utterance; something spoke out of me over

which I had no control.

'What?' said Mrs Reed under her breath: her usually cold, composed gray eye became troubled with a look like fear; she took her hand from my arm, and gazed at me as if she really did not know whether I were child or fiend. I was now in for it.

'My Uncle Reed is in heaven, and can see all you do and think; and so can papa and mamma: they know how you shut me up all day long, and how you wish me dead.'…..

Stories like Jane Eyre can be fine illustrations of righteousness and **self**-righteousness, and there is no harm using them as examples portraying injustices, as in this famous book. It may also be additional help for a fellow traveller in understanding the true meaning of righteousness and **self**-righteousness. Yes, God's Word, the Bible, explains it all perfectly well, but some authors go hand in hand with God's word, and, of course, Charlotte Bronte was a believer, as was her Jane Eyre.

It is a novel, beautifully written, emotional and intense; (a can't put downer!) with Christian morality within its lines. And though a child, Jane's outbursts were rightly justified, as ours would be if we were wrongly treated, though as adults, hopefully we would have learnt about 'the spirit of self control'!

It is so easy to criticize another for wrong behaviour, so we need to: **"First remove the plank from your own eye, and then you will see clearly to remove the speck from your brother's eye." Matthew 7:5.**

Yes, we are told in Scripture **Ephesians 4:26 Be angry and do not sin. Do not let the sun go down on your anger.** But Jane was ten years old and so very cruelly treated and perhaps she wasn't aware of her anger being sin – or was it sin? If it was sin, then she was not righteous in her outbursts, but if her anger was justified, even as a child, then it would not be sin.

Jesus was righteously angry when he entered the temple to find people selling and buying. **Matthew 21:12-13 Then Jesus went into the temple of God and drove out all those who bought and sold in the temple, and overturned the tables of the money changers and the seats of those who sold doves. And He said to them. "It is written. 'My house shall be called a house of prayer, but you have made it a den of thieves.'"**

So we see there is 'justified righteousness' and when we are in the position to declare this ourselves, there is nothing wrong in doing so. There are those who have lost businesses because of their right up standing with God, just as those who leave their church for the same reason.

Let us take a look at **2 Corinthians 6:14-16. Do not be unequally yoked together with unbelievers. For what fellowship has righteousness with lawlessness? And what communion has light with darkness? And what accord has Christ with Belial? Or what part has a believer with an unbeliever? And what agreement has the temple of God with idols? For you are the temple of the living God. As God has said: "I will dwell in them and walk among them. I will be their God, and they shall be My people. Therefore, come out from among them and be separate," says the Lord. "Do not touch what is unclean, and I will receive you. I will be a Father to you. And you shall be My sons and daughters," says the Lord Almighty.**

Oh my goodness, where do we go from here? That sounds very harsh. Many of us have non Christian friends, non Christian children, parents, aunts, uncles, grandparents, cousins, nieces and nephews. Must we cut ourselves off from them? Do they live lawless lives? Do they live in darkness? We know that they are unbelievers. Must we separate ourselves from them?

Do we ask ourselves these important and searching questions? Most of us love our families, and many have difficulties with their relationships, so find they want to be separate from them because they don't 'get on'.

The demand to **'come out from among them, and be separate'** implies that we must not take part in any wrong activities with them. To give two simple examples: A friend invites you to watch, what you know to be, an unsuitable film, or perhaps asks you to join her in a 'fun' evening in a séance. As much as you like this friend and would want to please her by going, you know it is against all what you believe – you say you would rather not go. If she/he is a real friend and respects you, she will not argue and will accept your decision without further ado. In this you keep in right fellowship with God, pleasing Him rather than your friend.

A lot of us have non-believers as friends with whom we socialize and like very much, enjoying their company. Perhaps on the odd occasion we might be able to drop a relevant scripture verse or share a testimony. These little 'seeds' could be food for thought for them at a later date, but harm and intrusion hasn't shown its face! In this way we do not hide the fact that we are Christians, but very importantly do not announce ourselves as such. We can set a good example by just being the person we are made to be, and if anyone asks us if we believe in God or otherwise, make the best of this opportunity, but quietly. Christians can be very annoying and irritating by what comes across as dogmatism and it is very much a 'put off'. Experience speaks!

When Jesus on the shores of Galilee was preaching to thousands of people, He didn't shout, He didn't have to, even though there weren't microphones in His day. He spoke boldly and with authority, but the people had gathered to hear what He had to say, not for an afternoon of socializing. If we are socializing with unsaved friends, we are not there to preach, but simply that, to socialize, and who knows (as previously mentioned) an opportunity might present itself to share a testimony.

It is always a good idea before going out, to ask the Lord for His anointing and if there is to be anything He wants us to say with regards our faith. But let us always be expedient in the circumstances in which we find ourselves.

And so we separate ourselves from those who live in darkness by not partaking with them in the things that we know are not right. This attitude is **righteous** and not **self-righteous**; it is honouring to God.

It is also our duty to always pray for the unsaved. It is grievous to think that those we love and others in the world will perish, but prayer and praise are powerful and we need to take advantage of this power, daily, and at the same time acknowledging our own salvation – **For by grace you have been saved through faith, and that not of yourselves; it is a gift of God, not of works lest anyone should boast. Ephesians 2:8-9.**

<u>Of this we can be certain and be righteous in this certainty.</u>

FORGIVENESS AND UNFORGIVENESS

The following are three true episodes of forgiveness, which hopefully will stir the hearts of those who find forgiveness difficult, maybe even impossible.

Joan of Arc, when in 1412 was asked to deny that she received messages from God, and if she didn't, would be burnt to death. She loved Jesus so much that she chose death rather than denial. There were witnesses who claimed that they heard her forgive the people that had her executed unjustly.

Pope John Paul 2 suffered an attempted assassination by shooting in 1981 and was severely wounded. After his recovery the Pope visited his would be assassin in prison, spending time talking with him, and it is believed that the Pope forgave and prayed with him.

Therese of Lizeaux (known as the 'Little Flower') was born in 1873, and joined a French convent at the age of fifteen years old. Each morning whilst she was washing at a basin in a shared bathroom, another sister used to deliberately splash her. Therese never reacted and silently forgave her.

Therese's biography is written as 'The Story of a Soul.'

One may perceive this last episode as not particularly important, perhaps even a silly example. "So what! No big deal being splashed." (Take note, it was every morning.)

'Silly' incidences like these are a common occurrence in every day life, with people usually retaliating in one way or another, thus causing resentment, which damages something within us. Little annoyances in our lives are important enough for us with which to deal. If left, they can easily have a gangrene affect on ourselves and others. We might not be aware of this.

A neighbour's footballs continually come over into your garden; at first you throw them back, but soon the situation becomes too much, so you stop returning them. They eventually pile up and you decide to burn them. Not only would you be burning the footballs, but part of your soul and that of your neighbours. "Serve them right", you think. Does it really?

A mature conversation to begin with would have been sensible, explaining your annoyance and frustration. If the situation didn't change, had you thought about prayer? "No! How does one pray for something like that?" You would be surprised at the power of prayer for 'something like that.'! We forgive those who trespass against us.

Let us not undermine the power of prayer. Jesus is not only interested in the big things in life – illness, divorce, adultery, imprisonment, but the so called little, seemingly unimportant things, are His to take care of as well.

It is wrong for Christians to go through life with grudges of un- forgiveness. Forgiveness is that which Jesus gave us from the cross. It was His gift to us, and we need to accept it graciously and with whole hearted thanks, and use as was intended. It frees the spirit. We need to also remember, that unless we forgive, we cannot be forgiven. **Matthew 6:15. "But if you do not forgive men their trespasses, neither will your Father forgive your trespasses."**

The parable of the prodigal son is a fine example of forgiveness, when it is given in generous doses by the son's father, who greets him with one thought. **"This son of mine was dead, but now he is alive, he was lost, but now has been found."** Luke 15:15-32.

Sadly to say, the prodigal's brother held resentment and was not forgiving toward his reckless, wasteful and extravagant sibling.

There was a teacher at a particular school who showed, unwittingly, an act of forgiveness. She was standing with a mother and her son, and having been told of his misconduct, the mother asked him what he should say. He immediately said that he was sorry. The teacher radiated a smile, put out her hand and shook his, saying, 'I forgive you…'. This incident is a wonderful illustration of the teacher's readiness to forgive, her smile, her handshake - all showing a warm spirit of forgiveness. What a fine example to a child.

There are times when we need to stand back and take a look at ourselves, maybe consider the prayer from **Psalm 139:23-24, Search me O God and know my heart and see if there is any wicked way in me and lead in the way everlasting.**

Perhaps recall how we felt at the time we were offended or when we offended someone. Were we sorry? Did we apologise. Did they accept? If we were not in the wrong, did the other apologise? Did we accept? What were the feelings and attitudes afterwards? It is good to think upon these things as it helps us to consider our frame of mind towards others and theirs towards us.

"I will never forgive him/her/them," are words often spoken by those who have been hurt in some 'unforgivable' way. They do not see the sense of forgiving and decide to hold a grudge, not realising that this way of thinking harms only themselves – because they have to live with themselves, and so will always be weighed down with dislike or hatred.

It is not always easy to forgive, but it is wise to 'try to want to' - before it eats us up.

God has a way of softening people's hearts. **Ezekiel 36:26 says when God talks to Ezekiel with regard Israel – "I will give you a new heart and put a new spirit within you. I will take the heart of stone out of your flesh and give you a heart of flesh. I will put my Spirit within you and cause you to walk in my statutes, and you will keep my judgements and do them."**

To refer to the cross again. **Luke 23:34 "Forgive them Father! They know not what they do."**

Jesus had hung on the cross for hours, in agony from the nails in His hands and feet, and beforehand, the flogging, spitting and hitting and the placing of thorns on His head. The fiercest pain He endured was the sins of the world – our sins. Here He was atoning for our wrong doings so as we might be set free. Is it much to ask for us to forgive all the petty actions and words in which we indulge ourselves? So often we need to get our lives into perspective and see what we are about.

Colossians 3:12-13 therefore as the elect of God, holy and beloved, put on tender mercies, kindness, humbleness of mind, meekness, long-suffering; bearing with one another, and forgiving one another, if anyone has a complaint against another; even as Christ forgave you, so you also must do.

The Lord's prayer which was given to mankind from Jesus Himself, tells us how we should pray. The part where it says, 'forgive us our trespasses as we forgive those who trespass against us' says it all.

Have you ever asked this question? - why didn't God forgive Adam and Eve? Maybe it was because of their attitude. There was no apology, just blame; they played the 'blame game'. Adam accused Eve and Eve accused the snake. If only they had had remorse, God, no doubt, would have readily forgiven them, but there was none of it. We have to regret our misconduct and apologise for it if we are to have spirits in Christ, as well as accepting apologies from those who aggrieve us.

Matthew 18:21-22 Then Peter came to Him and said, Lord, how often shall my brother sin against me, and I forgive him? Up to seven times? Jesus said to him. "I do not say to you up to seven times, but up to seventy times

seven..." He then tells them the parable of the unforgiving servant – Matthew 18:25-28.

What about those who die before we have made our peace with them, leaving us with the knowledge that there was never forgiveness between us? It is awful and extremely sad. Let us take a look at **Ephesians 4:25-28 Therefore, putting away lying, each one speak truth with his neighbour, for we are members of one another. <u>Be angry and do not sin, do not let the sun go down on your wrath</u>, nor give place to the devil.**

How many of us go to bed having had a disagreement of some sort with a spouse, a child or a friend, closing our eyes before setting things right?

There is a story of a couple who had had a row, the last words spoken by one were "Go to Hell." The other hearing these words died as a result of a car accident that day. We must be at peace with everyone all the time, and if we are unable to be, at least the effort to make it should be in our hearts.

Martin Luther King had a word to say on forgiveness: "Forgiveness is not an occasional act, it is a constant attitude."

An unforgiving spirit is like a poison that runs through us. It not only blocks out connection with offenders and the offended, but most of all with God. As with our fellow humans, when a relationship breaks down, it often leaves bitterness and resentment. It causes unhappiness and is very draining, particularly if one is a Christian with an understanding of un- forgiveness.

A certain person had been in this state for a year - a Christian with a bitter and resentful spirit. The Holy Spirit spoke to his soul, saying he must 'do something kind for the person he was resenting.' He was quite shocked at this request, but acquiesced, and was immediately set free. Since, he has been learning a lot about not holding onto resentments.

John 13:26 "If anyone serves me, let him follow me; and where I am there my servant shall be also. If anyone serves me, him my Father will honour."

1 Samuel 2:30 Therefore the Lord God of Israel says, "I said indeed that your house and the house of your father would walk before me for ever." but now the Lord says. "Far be it from me; for those who honour me I will honour, and those who despise me shall be lightly esteemed."

A few years ago, a lady lost her child through a terrorist bombing. One cannot imagine the grief she suffered and can understand the hatred in her heart towards the killers. She was unable to forgive them at the time, so felt to leave her church. A very honourable and admirable decision. Her family and friends loved and protected her, so she was able to live on as best she could. Does she still have that unforgiving heart, we might ask. Would we blame her if she had? We need to pray for this broken hearted mother, that one day she will be able to let go and allow God to deal with this tragic event. Forgiveness does set us free and it is possible. Sometimes it takes a few minutes, sometimes hours, sometimes days, months or even years. There is no doubt that those praying for the heart to forgive, are forgiven, having received the strength Jesus promises us when we are weak. **1Corinthians 12:9a…. And He said to me, "My grace is sufficient for you, for my strength is made perfect in weakness…."**

He heals the broken hearted and binds up their wounds. Psalm 147:3

It would be good to read the whole Psalm as it is full of praise for our Mighty God, and this indeed is what He wants us to do and we should want to do as well, even when in our humanity we don't always feel like it!

One of the greatest human stories in the history of the Bible on forgiveness, is the one of Joseph and his brothers. First, what jealousy can do, then fear, and finally forgiveness. It makes a fascinating read. **Genesis 37-50.**

Let us remember that forgiveness is a wonderful and generous gift. It is one we should receive with thanksgiving and praise to our God and His Son Jesus, always cherishing it in our hearts and learning to use it - **"not occasionally, but with a constant attitude."**

BLASPHEMY

The Ten Commandments were given to Moses by God nearly 1,500 years before Christ. Two thousand plus years after Christ, they are still here, written down for people to read – in the Bible. They are seldom, if ever, preached on. Too old fashioned?

They were still a significant part of life in this nation up until the mid 20th century, though slowly but surely taking a back seat, being ignored or side lined.

Pushing God out was the beginning of the fall of what was once a Christian nation. Since, morals and values, which were once respected and honoured, have mostly vanished from society. Even those who did not embrace the Christian faith lived within its boundaries to a certain degree. People are now complacent, just accepting these changes without much as a 'how y'do', and many showing hostility toward Christians.

The masses cried out for changes in God's Laws, and they were granted. In the Old Testament, the masses cried out for Saul to be King and their cries were answered. **1Samuel 8**. We were given free wills, and God at times gives what we ask for, though injurious to us.

We were once hung and beheaded for making a stand for our beliefs, now we lose our jobs, are ridiculed and considered weird. This hostility, however, is the 'cross' Christians have to, or choose to, carry for their faithfulness.

John 16:18-19 "If the world hates you, you know that it hated me before it hated you. If you were of the world, the world would love its own. Yet because you are not of the world, but I chose you out of the world, therefore the world hates you."

This short narrative is about one of the Ten Commandments. **Exodus 20, the 2nd Commandment. "You shall not take the name of the Lord God in vain, for the Lord will not hold him guiltless who takes His name in vain."**

The blasphemy laws were repealed in England and Wales in July 2008 and abolished the same year. The government apparently had consulted the Church of England, and they urged them to go ahead. So much for the Church!

What can we do about it?

We can pray. Prayer is for ever powerful, alongside with praise. There are hymns old, and new, with words of praise for us to sing; modern choruses echo the same. Praise is always joyful and reverent; at times solemn and deep; always wonderful and uplifting. It rises as a sweet aroma to God in heavenly places; it satisfies His heart, blessing Him abundantly.

Many Psalms are songs of praise. They tell us of David, Israel's great King, how he loved God, sought Him in times of difficulty, trusted Him and forever hoped in Him, praising Him for all His wonders and just for who He is.

There was once a little girl who always believed in God. She knew of Jesus, but didn't know Him personally. She used to cringe on hearing God's name being used as a swear word. She must have sensed in her spirit that it was wrong to be used in this way. Though unaware that He was a Holy God, she knew His Name was special. Now an adult, she knows Jesus and reads His Word, she understands why she cringed, and though she still cringes when hearing His named blasphemed, she now praises it. (something she didn't know to do as a child.)

How dare people drag this beautiful Name through the mud of their lives, disrespecting it, saying it as a swear word. Yes, swear words are vulgar and offensive, but better they are used than His Name.

However, there is a however, and it is this: one has to remember that many do not know what they are saying. We need to turn to the Cross in our thoughts and think of the enemies of Jesus who were cursing Him as He hung dying. **"Forgive them Father, for they know not what they do."** were the words of Jesus. **Luke 23:34.**

Consequently, we must have a righteous attitude, and pray for those who 'do not know what they do', asking God's forgiveness, and for the Holy Spirit to make them aware.

Paul, the writer of many books in the New Testament was a known blasphemer, but my, how God loved him, forgave him, and used him tremendously. **Although I was formerly a blasphemer, a persecutor, and an insolent man; I obtained mercy because I did it ignorantly in unbelief. 1 Timothy 13.**

Paul quotes from **Deuteronomy 32:35 "Vengeance is mine and recompense….."** Why did God say this? Because the Israelites had turned their backs on Him and worshipped other gods.

But because God decided to send His Son Jesus to make recompense for our sins, instead of being vengeful, we have to learn to love, and by loving that means forgiving and praying for those who offend God, remembering that He forgives immediately those who really repent. There is tremendous power in forgiveness which we know by the Cross.

There are those who claim that there isn't a God, and yet they curse Him beyond measure. To quote one individual: "Why should I respect a capricious, mean minded and stupid God?" If the Law of Blasphemy had not been abolished, perhaps this person would be in prison today, and many others of similar ilk. Or maybe not!

The last successful conviction was in the early 1960s when a student newspaper was fined for satirizing the New Testament. The last person to be hung for blasphemy was in Scotland in 1697, because he denied the veracity of the Old Testament and the legitimacy of Christ's miracles.

Isaiah 26:10 Let grace be shown to the wicked, yet he will not learn righteousness; in the land of uprightness he deals unjustly, and will not behold the majesty of the Lord.

Yes, men curse God, even the God some do not believe in! It is all around us and on the television and social media. There is a total lack of respect by the ignorant for the God who created us in His own image.

There were times when David wished death to the enemy – human as he was, and like many in the world today, he wished vengeance on those who offended him. **Psalm 139:19-22** tells us that he asked God to slay the wicked and how he hated them.

We are told in Romans **12:19-21 Beloved do not avenge yourselves, but rather give place to wrath; for it is written "Vengeance is mine, I will repay" says the Lord. Therefore if your enemy hungers, feed him; if he thirsts give him a drink; for in doing you will heap coals of fire on his head. Do not be overcome by evil but overcome evil with good.**

David loved to praise the Lord, and in **Samuel 6:14** we read.. **then David danced before the Lord.**

In **Samuel 13:14** That he was a man after God's own heart - **The Lord sort for Himself a man after His own heart...**

In **Acts 13:22** Paul tells us that after God had removed Saul....**He raised for them David as King, to who also He gave testimony and said, "I have found David the son of Jesse, a man after my own heart who will do all my will."**

Since the fall of man men have battled against each other, against God, against Jesus. Men who don't believe, however, do not battle against the evil one as Christians do. However, we must remember that the battle belongs to the Lord. **2Chronicles 20 Do not be afraid or dismayed, for the battle belongs to the Lord as we wrestle against the spiritual forces of evil.**

And let us never forget that He is always with us **"...and lo, I am with you always, even to the end of the age." Matthew 28:20.** There are plenty of Bible verses telling us this, and that we are also over comers. **Little children, you are from God and have overcome them, for He who is in you is greater than he who is in the world. 1John 4:4.**

There are further forms of blasphemy other then taking His name in vain. Bibles are thrown away, even burned. They are ridiculed – and to think that there are more Bibles sold in the world than any other book. That has to say something! His Word is undoubtedly a threat to unbelievers; it challenges them, making them angry and defiant.

People take the 'mickey' out of Christian beliefs in stage plays, films and television. God is mocked in many ways.

Jesus, Himself, was accused of blasphemy. **Matthew 9:3... And at once some of the scribes said within themselves, "This man blasphemes!"**

If this accusation wasn't so serious, it would be laughable. Jesus accused of cursing! - and because He healed a sick man and forgave him his sins.

Despite all the teachings over the three years they walked with Him, His disciples found it difficult to believe that He was the Messiah. However, they did not curse Him; they loved Him, admired Him and followed Him as best they could throughout their doubting and their confusion.

How wonderful and blessed are we who have been enlightened by His Holy Spirit. **"Blessed are those who have not seen and yet have believed." John 20:29.**

Blasphemy is outrageous. We need to know, understand, and remember that it is a curse against our heavenly Father. It is not to be taken lightly, and we need to get into the habit of praising His Name when we hear it being cursed.

OMG is used on social media frequently. Yes, the writer might be saying, 'O my goodness', but there are those who are not. The name of Jesus is defamed in most every day conversations. Why? Pure ignorance? Yes, a lot of the time, and this is of the evil one who wants this magnificent Name not to be known as the Son of God.

As Christians, too, we much watch our own tongues.

His Name is Wonderful, Councillor, Mighty God, Everlasting Father and The Prince of Peace. Jesus, the only Name given unto man whereby a man can be saved. Isaiah 9:6.

These words are used in a hymn - (lyrics (c) Manna Music) and it is a triumphal hymn to listen to and sing. God is recognised exactly as that – Wonderful, Counsellor, Mighty

God, Everlasting Father, The Prince of Peace. He is the Great Shepherd, the Mighty King, the Rock, our salvation. He is Jesus our Lord. We worship and praise His holy name.

Our Father, who art in heaven,

HALLOWED BE THY NAME,

Thy Kingdom come,

Thy will be done on earth,

As it is in heaven.

Give us this day our daily bread,

And forgive us our trespasses,

As we forgive those who trespass against us.

And lead us not into temptation,

But deliver us from evil. AMEN.

Yes, His Name is to be Hallowed, not blasphemed, and by writing this and passing it on, it is a source of relaying the message.

BE HOLY AS I AM HOLY

TEMPTATION

'Lead us not into temptation' is taken from the Lord's prayer, or as is commonly know, The Our Father.

When we ask the Father to 'lead us not into temptation', that is just what He will do – not lead us into temptation.

Asking God not to lead us into temptation is a wise ask, believing and knowing that He won't. God does not allow any temptation to overtake us.

1Corinthians 10:13 No temptation has overtaken you except such as is common to man; but God is faithful, who will not allow you to be tempted beyond what you are able, but with the temptation will also make the way of escape, that you may be able to bear it.

Temptation is all around us; we live in a kingdom which is not of God. Jesus said it Himself in **John 18:36 …. "My kingdom is not of this world. If my kingdom were of this world, my servants would fight, so I should not be delivered to the Jews; but now my kingdom is not from here."**

When Satan, who was once an angel, was thrust out of God's presence, he became ruler of this world. His hatred is so deep, it surpasses anything else, and his determination to destroy and fill hell with as many souls as possible is indeterminate. Thus our ask of Jesus, 'lead us not into temptation but deliver us from evil.' is just that – to let not us to be tempted in ways that surpass us. And in this He has promised we wouldn't be.

James 4:7-8 therefore submit to God. Resist the devil and he will flee from you. Draw near to God and He will draw near to you …. and Jeremiah 29:11-13…. "for I know the thoughts that I think towards you" says the Lord, "thoughts of peace and not of evil, to give you a future and a hope. Then you will call upon me and go and pray to me, and I will listen to you. And you will seek me and find me when you search for me with all your heart…"

Wonderful words of encouragement and **1Peter 5:8-9 tells us: to be sober, be vigilant; because your adversary the devil walks about like a roaring lion, seeking who he may devour. Resist him, steadfast in the faith, knowing that the same sufferings are experienced by your brotherhood in the world.**

Knowing that this world to be Satan's kingdom assists us in our turning away from the things that entice us, which we know to be not of God.

Adam and Eve were tempted by Satan in the garden, with him telling them that they would be like God and know all things if they ate of the Tree of Life. They succumbed - to their detriment and ours.

Today the 'fruit' comes in other guises, and because the serpent is still as cunning as ever, and still a whisperer of lies, we are so easily magicked into believing him.

The media is a good example, where viewers are tempted to watch supposedly harmless programmes – those which feed wrong ideas into the thoughts of gullible and vulnerable minds. Social media used incorrectly, is known to have destroyed the lives of many adults and children, as have smart phones and apps. of various kinds. Where immorality is dressed up as the norm, then we have to have the courage of our convictions, (having first been convicted) which is our belief in a Holy God, and do an about turn, refusing to be fed by unsuitable media and television.

When the Pharisees asked Jesus if it was lawful to pay taxes to Caesar, He asked for a coin and asked the questions: **"Whose head is this and whose inscription?" And they answered, "Caesar's."** His reply was very clear. **"Render**

therefore to Caesar the things that are Caesar's, and to God the things that are God's." Matthew 22:21.

So, too, when we are faced with temptation, let us allow ourselves to ponder on whatever it is we are tempted by and turn our minds to scripture. We eventually will learn that it is so much better to leave the things of the world to those who want them and where they belong. The pull of the flesh is a daily experience, and this should encourage us to have a deeper and more meaningful relationship with Jesus. Because we are flesh, there will always be a strong pull towards the things of the flesh. However, being born of the spirit, our pull to the things of the spirit hopefully overrides the other.

Finally, brethren, whatever things are true, whatever things are noble, whatever things are just, whatever things are pure, whatever things are lovely, whatever things are of good report, if there is any virtue and if there is anything praise worthy – meditate on these things. The things which you learned and received and heard and saw in me, these do, and the God of peace will be with you. Philippians 4:8. Great advice!

We have to discipline ourselves daily. God wants us to be holy, as He is holy, and though it may take a long time, we need to persevere. Let us not see it as a burden, and keep in mind that our perseverance is pleasing to God. We carry our imperfections with us, so you may ask, how do we achieve 'be perfect, as I am perfect'? Let us not be intransigent. When we are faced with temptation, we can be weakened in our resolve to turn our backs on it but we need to learn to respect God and ourselves. God is ever faithful. His Word and His promises never change. **Jesus Christ is the same yesterday, today and forever. Hebrews 13:8.**

It is man that changes – like a chameleon - and perhaps the reason is, that he quite often prefers to please himself and others rather than God. Jesus was in the desert for six weeks, spending time with His Father, and Satan came to Him with temptations that could have beguiled Him. After all He must have been very hungry, and could easily have turned the stones into bread as Satan smugly suggested He do; then to throw Himself down from the pinnacle of the temple, to trust the angels would look after Him, and finally to bow down and worship him. The audacity!

Matthew 4:3-11 -To the first Jesus replied, **"Man shall not live by bread alone, but by every word that proceeds from the mouth of God."**

To the second: **"It is written again, 'You shall not tempt the Lord your God.'"**

To the third: **"Away with you Satan! For it is written 'You shall worship the Lord your God and Him only shall you serve.'"**

And as we have already read, God gives us away of escape.

There is no need for us to conform to the pattern of our society when we know it is not God's way. When we are tempted to join others in watching inappropriate television, talk in unfitting ways, agree with things that we know are not right, just to protect ourselves, it is good to be able to handle these and other unsuitable situations in a mature and sensible manner.

Remember Jesus is closer to us than the air we breathe, so just a whisper of 'help' is sufficient. Silence is golden in circumstances where someone is talking of another in an unkind manner. It is easy to agree with the gossiper just so as not to appear to be a 'goody goody'. It is a betrayal of the person being gossiped about, even though what was said is true. It is kinder not to say anything at all, or perhaps respond with something positive about him/her. Most people have a good side to them! But if you are not aware of this side, then silence has to be golden.

We all like justice, and in order to obtain it when we are

misrepresented, we quite often are tempted to acquire it through incorrect means. This temptation must be avoided, as it usually leads one into sin. We need to pray that justice will be done, for it is God who justifies.

Romans 8:33-34 Who shall bring a charge against God's elect? It is He who justifies. Who is He who condemns? It is Christ who died, and further more is also risen, who is even at the right hand of God, who also makes intercession for us.

It would be worthwhile reading through to the end of the chapter.

Joseph in **Genesis 39** was tempted by Pharaoh's wife, but he resisted, and imprisoned for something he didn't do.

David was tempted to kill Saul – **1 Samuel 24** – he restrained himself knowing that Saul was God's anointed; but in **2 Samuel 11**, he was tempted when seeing Bathshepa on a balcony, and lust overcame him; he succumbed, committed adultery and then murder!

So as we pray 'lead us not into temptation', and when walking in God's will, He will do just that - not lead us into temptation. We need to stay close to Him and He will stay close to us every mini second of every twenty four hours.

Trust in His faithfulness, honour Him, praise Him and love Him.

Watch and pray, lest you enter into temptation. The spirit is indeed willing, but the flesh is weak. Matthew 26:41.

WHAT IS THE PURPOSE OF LIFE?

The title makes for a loaded question when we ask ourselves seriously – what really <u>is</u> the purpose of life? especially asked by those without a faith. Why am I here, what am I doing here on earth?

One is able to fully understand the non-Christian asking this, after all he thinks and believes that ultimately we simply pop off from this life, we are gone forever, poof, the end of our humanity. For the Christian though, it is the end of our humanity on earth, it is also the beginning of our total spirituality, living with our Father in another world, the spiritual world, until Jesus comes again to take our new resurrected bodies into a new heaven and a new earth.

Sadly to say in the non-Christian world there are many who take their own lives because they do not have hope, but despair, and when one despairs, one takes drastic measures. Having not known their Creator, having not known their Saviour, life seems to be a bottomless pit of sorrow, personal and worldly, so why hang around waiting – waiting for what? I suppose death. So instead of waiting, they embrace it themselves.

For the Christian the purpose of life is first to love God with our whole heart, soul and strength. (The first commandment – **Matthew 22:37-40.**)

How do we love God and our Saviour? That is a question that can only be answered by those who actually have the Spirit of God living inside of them. There is no other way. If one asks an atheist why she/he doesn't believe in God, the answer is usually, 'Well, if there is a God, why does He allow all the suffering in the world.' We, as Christians, may have asked, 'What is the purpose of life?' especially when we are going through bad times of a sort, and not understanding why.

The following verse in the Bible might help, that though they believe, find themselves doubting.

Jeremiah 18:5-6 "Oh house of Israel, can I not do with you as this potter?" says the Lord. "Look, as the clay is in the potter's hand, so are you in my hand, O house of Israel..." Just so, we are in God's hand, and He moulds us into shape day by day, month by month, year by year. At times cracks appear, at times certain amounts of clay have to be removed or added so as to make sure we are being moulded correctly, and it is at these points in our lives when we feel, maybe battered, forgotten, hurt, and think that everything is now pointless; what is the use of going on! But go on we must and go on we hopefully do, only to realise sooner or later that God always knows what He is doing, and that doing is for our best. Let us praise Him!

From the first sin of Adam, mankind has suffered. The first murder, we can read in **Genesis 4:1-16**, tells us of the jealousy Cain felt toward Able. Jealousy is always described as being 'green with envy', envy being similar to jealousy. (Apparently sins are identified by colours!) And because of his deep outrageous jealousy Cain was driven to kill his brother. And so this has continued throughout human history.

God's Son, Jesus, was also murdered, but in a more brutal way, and though the reason for Him being crucified was because He claimed to be the Son of God, it was also because He had to die to take the punishment for our sins, so as we, the human race could be set free. Could God have done it some other way, one might ask. Yes, I am sure He could have, but as His ways are not our ways and His thoughts not our thoughts, **(Isaiah 55:8-9)** He chose this distinct means to redeem mankind.

And who are we to question Him? **Romans 9:20 But indeed, O man, who are you to reply against God? Shall the thing formed say to Him who formed it, "Why have you made me like this?"** and Isaiah humbly says, **"But now, O Lord, you are our Father, we are the clay, and you are the potter, we are all the work of Your hand.**

Knowing and believing this offers Christians amazing peace – that peace that passes all understanding.

Phillipians 4:7 and **John 14:7** Jesus says, **"Peace I leave with you; my peace I give to you. <u>I do not give to you as the world gives. Do not let your hearts be troubled; do not be afraid</u>."** (underlining mine)

We can conclude from this that those who do not believe, rely on the things of the world to give them comfort and peace. As Christians we rely on Him, the source of our peace.

It is urgently recommended that we pray for those who do not believe that they have a Saviour. Many are cynics, but God can change the hardest heart. We only have to look at Paul of the New Testament! If ever there was a cynical unbeliever he sure was! There must have been those praying for him as he went about brutally punishing individuals who claimed Jesus as the Messiah.

In society today, Christians who make a stand for their beliefs are castigated in many ways, so though punishment has changed in our part of the world, the human race hasn't and is still as murderous in their hearts, if not occasionally, in actuality, as they were 2000 years ago and since the beginning of creation.

The purpose of life for the ordinary citizen is just to live it out. Many are kind, compassionate, understanding and loving folk, who want to do their best for each and everyone. Then, why, the question arises, will they go to a lost eternity after they die? It seems terribly unfair, especially when they might have had a better attitude toward others than those who claim to be Christian. To put this into perspective with a simple explanation - if you become a member of a particular club, and having paid the required subscription, the club is open to you. If you are not a valid member, than you are not allowed access to the club. Is this fair? The same principle applies to the non-believer going to a lost eternity; having never accepted Christ as his/her Redeemer, never believed in God, so he/she cannot enter into the Kingdom of Heaven. We all have choices, as hard as it may seem, remembering too that: **the righteous requirement of the law might be fulfilled in us** who <u>do not walk according to the flesh but according to the Spirit</u>...Romans 8:5 (underlining mine)

Thus it is so vital to pray for the salvation of souls. There <u>is</u> hope for <u>everyone</u>.

John3:16 For God so loved the world that He gave His only begotten Son, that whoever believes in Him should not perish, but have everlasting life.

And as it is written in **1Timothy 2:1-5 Therefore I exhort first of all that <u>supplications, prayers, intercessions, and giving of thanks be made for all men, for kings and all who are in authority</u> that we lead a quiet and peaceable life in all godliness and reverence. For this is good and acceptable in the sight of God our Saviour, <u>who desires all men to be saved and to come to the knowledge of the truth</u>.** (underlining mine)

There we have it in black and white – God loves mankind, He grieves, and is rightfully angry at their disbelief, their arrogance and disobedience. We only have to read about the Israelites when rescued from Egypt – their total hubris, their making of another god, their worshipping it, wanting to do their own thing.

Exodus 32 makes a worthwhile read.

We need leadership, someone who can lead the lost sheep into the green pastures that are promised to us by the Good Shepherd. Moses led the Israelites through the desert for forty years, which could have been eleven days, or thereabouts, but because of their continual intransigence, plus Moses himself who so often complained they were their own worst enemy. Finally Joshua was appointed leader. He was a non-complaining prophet who got on with the job allocated to him, thus he came into the promised land – those green pastures of milk and honey!

(Suggest to read the **Book of Joshua**.)

Let us remember however, that we must learn to be faithful in 'little things.' as well. **Luke 16:10 "He who is faithful in what is least is faithful also in much; and he who is unjust in what is least in unjust also in much."**

The majority of Christians are unknown, just ordinary people, going about their daily lives. Their lives appear to be quite insignificant. But to God, no life is insignificant. Every life is precious and important – from the murderer, the liar, the rapist, and the debaucher; and the prestigious, such as preachers, teachers, missionaries, journalists, doctors and many other prominent people. Conventional individuals simply 'bloom where they are planted.' But to 'bloom' is important. The purpose for this 'blooming' is to spread the Gospel effectively. As we are not all called to be preachers in church, or on 'Speaker's Corner', we are asked to be bringers of the Good News in our every days lives whenever possible.

Those who are non-believers, having a more optimistic view on life than those who hate the believer, one could say are better off, feeling fulfilled in general. There is nothing wrong in that, in fact far better than being pessimistic, resentful. But, of course, the sadness is that they too will be lost souls. They desperately need to know and understand that their purpose for this life is to know their Saviour and to share eternity with Him.

We read in the **Book of Ecclesiastes 3:11** that God has put eternity in every man's heart. **He has made everything beautiful in its time. Also he has put eternity in their hearts, except that no one can find out the work that God does from beginning to end.**

If we look around us, we can see and sense that man, generally, is not really completely satisfied with life. There is always an uncertainty in his heart if he is really cares to admit it. And in the rich this is decidedly present.

'What is the purpose of my life', no doubt has to be the thought of many rich people in the world - those who can have anything and everything they want – they are never really content, always reaching out for new things, hoping whatever it is will finally bring what they believe, unconsciously, the contentment they so long for. But it never happens.

Let us take another look at **Ecclesiastes**; in fact it would be a good idea to read the whole book. It is quite short with only twelve chapters. But the one which is worth pointing out here is **Chapter 11** under the heading **'Seek God in Early Life.' Rejoice O young man, in your youth, and let your heart cheer you in the days of your youth. Walk in the ways of your heart, and in the sight of your eyes. <u>But know that for all these God will bring you into judgement. Therefore remove sorrow from your heart and put away evil from your flesh, for childhood and youth are vanity</u>.** (underlining mine)

Unfortunately Christians quite often are a threat to the heathen. Why? Is it that the unbeliever is afraid of the Truth, not knowing, of course, that if they had the Truth in their lives, they would be set free from all that bothers them and realise that they are loved mightily by their Creator?

They feel uncomfortable and don't wish to hear about beliefs. We must respect this, and do what we know we must and that is of course, pray. We know there is immense power in prayer, never to be underestimated.

Jesus tells us in **John 8:32 "And you shall know the Truth, and the Truth shall make you free."**

There was a lady, having lived a dreadful life, became a Christian, and one day after many years, met an old friend. Each asked the other how they were, and the lady who had converted related her testimony. The reply to this was; "If you think I want to spend eternity in heaven you have another think coming." She had sold her soul to the enemy and was a God hater. Perhaps there are many like her, but one would hope that the majority are not actually 'God haters' but simply do not have a belief. Nevertheless, this is still serious, and tragic, though, with a difference - there is still the possibility of them coming into faith.

What does all this boil down to? Can we honestly say that as Christians we know the purpose of our lives? Can the non-Christian really know the purpose of their lives?

The Christian's is to love God, and to take the Gospel to those who are not saved. The unsaved have a choice, just like we did. Their lives do not have a purpose in that they have nothing to live for, though, perhaps, their purpose is simply to live out this life as best they can.

So let us pray for the unbeliever, and know that …. **"there will be more joy in heaven over one sinner who repents than over ninety-nine just persons who need no repentance. Luke 15:7**

BE STILL AND KNOW THAT I AM GOD

Because the world is the way it is today, we need to be more and more aware of who we are in Christ and not get carried away by the world's activities, which are quite often disguised as being acceptable, a tactic of the evil one. We need to ask for wisdom – **James 1:5 If any of you lacks wisdom, let him ask of God, who gives liberally and without reproach, and it will be given to him.**

Be still and know that I am God Psalm 46:10.

To be still is to be quiet, to be in repose, to be mentally closed down to the world, to ourselves - to be focused on God. Is this really possible? There are times, it appears, that we are forced to take our quiet times in what might be unsuitable circumstances.

In the Old Testament Elisha was told to go, by the Lord, to the Brook Cherith. He was forced to be alone with God – no one else to chat or pray with, just God and himself. **1Kings 17:1-7**

As Elisha experienced – God was not in the wind, nor in the earthquake, nor in the fire, but in a still small voice. **1Kings 19:11-12.**

Again in the Old Testament, Joseph was imprisoned under Pharaoh, forced to be alone with God. **Genesis 41**.

God had far reaching plans for both these men, just as He has plans for us. Hopefully, we won't have to face such dire circumstances.

However, we might be forced to be alone with God, and it is in this unwilling enforcement that we will find Him waiting for us, waiting to speak to us face to face, heart to heart - this might be the only way He can get our attention and it is uncomfortable. As with many things in our lives, we have to learn to discipline ourselves, and quite often this in itself takes discipline.

In Mark 4:39 we read about Jesus calming the storm. One is able to imagine the 'beforehand', seemingly 'out of hand', the fierce sea, the disciples being tossed about in their boat, afraid that they would drown whilst Jesus slept. But Jesus wasn't concerned, He was 'still'. When they woke Him, He calmed the sea, **"Peace, be still,"** He said. **And the wind ceased and there was a great calm.** He says to us too, **"Peace, be still; why are you so fearful? How is it that you have no faith?"**

Our faith is depleted at times because we do not take that needed and special time out to 'be still', which allows us to 'know' that He is God.

When we come to realise that God is who He says He is, it is an awesome revelation. One can imagine Moses standing face to face with Him. **Exodus 34:29 Now it was so, when Moses came down from Mount Sinai (and the two tablets of the Testimony were in Moses' hand when he came down from the mountain), that Moses did not know that the skin of his face shone while he talked with Him.** Moses in his time of being alone on the mountain, got to 'know' his God, for he had been 'still'.

There are Christians whose faces shine with the glory of God, and have lived, and are still living in difficult circumstances. They spend time being 'still'.

We need to set time aside to be in His presence - to be still and know that He is God - even though we are in the shadow of His presence continually throughout each day and night.

When we go out walking on a calm day and there isn't a wind, or even a slight breeze, it is wonderful to feel the complete stillness. It can be quite breath taking just to stand with your eyes closed and to feel the stillness. It feels different, it is different. It is so calm that it wakes one up into thinking 'Wow, this is beautiful!' It can be so easily shrugged off as just a different day, lovely, but hey! But believe me, it is special, and it is so for a reason, so experience it, use it for acknowledging your Saviour; savour it.

In the stillness, God allows us to get to know Him. Yes, His thoughts are not our thoughts, and His ways are not our ways **Isaiah 55:8-9 "For my thoughts are not your thoughts, nor are your ways my ways," says the Lord.** but we come to know His splendour, His awesomeness, and to understand why His ways and thoughts are not the same as ours.

To know God is to believe in Him, is to have faith in Him, to love Him. We need to spend time in His Word as well, to get to know Him.

He wants us to share and fellowship with other Christians and this we are able to do within our prayer groups and gatherings at church. Some prayer groups may have a guitarist to accompany praise songs. In churches there are usually bands consisting of drums, keyboard and guitar, perhaps a flute or clashing cymbals, and occasionally a singer – all glorifying God – and God is blessed.

But, have we forgotten how to be the still, to be calm, to be silent?

Would we be able to spend time in silence in our prayer groups and in our church services? Could we sit, kneel, or stand for an hour in the quietness – without music?

We must know that a stage or platform is for performers, actors, so as they may be observed and hopefully enjoyed by the <u>audience</u> who have come to enjoy a concert; a group of people who have come to watch and listen. However, in church, the <u>congregation</u> are a group of people who have come together to <u>worship</u>.

With the bands being on stage, the congregation is distracted from worship because many, probably most, are checking out hair styles, shoes, make up, style, expressions…..quite a normal thing to do. You would have to be unusual and an exception to ignore all the performing artists in front of you.

This is not to decry their talents and sincerity in playing and singing, but are they not a distraction for the congregation, who are really - an audience?

It would need humility to go to one side or even to the back of the church and play and sing behind the worshippers, so as eyes and minds are less distracted and kept on Jesus.

The musicians and singers have a wonderful role to play

in church, providing accompaniment for the congregation. We are so used to having them that to try to sing acapella would not necessarily be welcome. However, wouldn't it be better judgement if they were in ear shot rather than eye shot?

In the traditional church and cathedral buildings, the organ is either at the side of the alter, or above, where only the organ pipes are visible. Now, however, musicians are invited to perform in front of the alter with a conductor conducting the singers. Truly lovely for a concert, but otherwise a distraction for worshippers.

These musically gifted people are very much recognised for their gifts; they are an integral part of church worship, always warmly welcomed and appreciated.

What about the musicians themselves? Are they distracted by their audience? Are they aware they may be seen as entertainers? We need to ask ourselves these questions, and without taking offence, so as to really know how we should function in church.

Another distraction is when folk divide into separate groups and during the time of prayer and discussion, there is back ground music. Thus so during the reading of notices.

The world also forces this onto us from the television and radio – music whilst someone is talking. Why? Surely the speaker would prefer our full attention?

The last months have been a wonderful opportunity for Christians to draw back from the world. In fact, we have been <u>forced</u> to do so. It has been a time to look at ourselves and ask God to search our hearts – **Search me, O God and know my heart; Try me and know my anxieties; And see if there is any wicked way in me, and lead me in the way everlasting. Psalm 139:23-24.**

We have no option but to be in the world, but it is not an option to be of it. This is difficult, as the world is all around us in various guises, tempting us to partake of its fruits - the television and the digital paraphernalia with all that they entail - and it is up to us to practice common sense and to keep a balance in their usability - so honouring God.

Censorship is important as was once thought by the government. No longer are our films censored, and though particular facets on Face time and certain apps. are, on the whole there is very little censorship.

God is a Holy God, and He asks that we be holy; actually, He demands it. **1Peter 1:15-16. But as He who called you is holy, you also be holy in all your conduct, because it is** written. **"Be holy, for I am holy."**

To learn how to be as He wants us to be, we need to be 'still' within the body, as well as in our private times.

We need to always remain teachable, not to be 'know alls', but humble in learning God's ways. We have to pursue holiness, and as we do, we would soon begin to perceive our sins of intolerance, demands and other offences. Peter in **Luke 5:8** recognised his own sin when he saw the Holiness of Jesus, and in a rush of humility he exclaimed: **Depart from me, for I am a sinful man, O Lord.** Are we able to exclaim the same? Peter's impetuous nature and his impatience, however, did not stop him from pursuing holiness.

Zacchaeus too, acknowledging the Holiness of Jesus, pursued in his determination to give up his old rebellious life. We can imagine him running around in great excitement paying back all his debts, and more, desiring nothing else but to follow the Man who saw his sin and forgave him! **Luke 19:1-10.** (His name actually means 'clean'!)

Paul, not having met Jesus in the flesh, but in the Spirit, pursued holiness, and encourages us to do so.

We do not have to be great characters in order to pursue

holiness. We just have to be God's people. Jesus sees our sins; we cannot hoodwink Him, so let us too pursue holiness in such a way that it will take precedence over everything that would stand in our way.

God uses disciples and prophets to demonstrate His Greatness, His Power, His Holiness, altogether His Character and His purposes. There are untold numbers of Peters, Zachaeuss and Pauls today who will never be known, except to God alone, for their pursuit of holiness. The importance is that they pursued.

We really have to be in line with His will. Surely then with this in mind, we must be a people set apart, and the more set apart we are, the more God is able to act in our lives, giving us the ability to change anything that needs changing.

If anyone reading this has ever been in love, you may remember how you longed for the company of the one you loved. You wanted to be alone with one another; you just wanted to talk and to listen to each other; you took an interest in the other's day to day life. Maybe you phoned your love one during the day, wanting to hear his/her voice; you couldn't wait to meet up again; the days and nights seemed interminable.

So we should love Jesus. In our day to day activities we are not necessarily aware of His continual presence; it is only when we stop for a moment and think, do we become conscious of Him. But, we can add to this recognition by taking that well needed, and hopefully wanted, time out, away from our daily recreation, and learn to 'be still and know that He is God.'

Do you ever wonder how anyone cannot believe in our Creator? When you look around and consciously notice flowers, grasses, trees, water, birds, earth worms, blue skies, grey skies, the rain, the frost, hail, snow and so many other extraordinary wonders in the world; the seas, the mountains. None of these are man made, some may have evolved over the years in size, colour, or shape, but ultimately, everything on earth was made by His hand, His Breath. The best of all was man, and after man the baby. I am sure you have looked at a new baby – the hands, the fingers and nails, the ears, nose and mouth. The noises babies make – all so amazing - **I am fearfully and wonderfully made, marvellous are your works so says David in Psalm 139:14a.**

We only have to read **Genesis 1:1-2** to know our Creator is God. The world scientists have nothing on God. He was, and is, the greatest scientist that ever existed. **"I am the**

Mary Marriott

Alpha and the Omega, the Beginning and the End, says the Lord, **"Who is and Who was and Who is to come, the Almighty." Revelation 1:8.**

Let us take advantage of any and every opportunity given to us to: BE STILL - AND KNOW - THAT HE IS GOD

ONE HOUR AND THE TEN COMMANDMENTS

Let us rejoice in the Lord. Let us thank Him for Himself, for His creation, for His faithfulness, for His energetic love, for His heart breaking love in sending Jesus, His Son, to suffer because of the sin of disobedience.

Why is mankind punished because of what someone else did? Isn't that totally unfair? God's ways are not our ways has to be a constant reminder of things we do not understand. That is what is so wonderful about having the Holy Spirit living inside of us. We simply believe and accept all that God does and doesn't do.

As it is written in **Jeremiah 18** when God was referring to Israel - **Verse 6b. "Can I not do with you as this potter?" says the Lord. "Look, as the clay is in the potter's hand, so are you in My hand. O house of Israel."**

We, too, are in God's hand. Don't let us shrink from this truth and try to escape. We should rejoice that He loves us as He does, and allow Him to mould us as a potter moulds his clay into whatever design he has in mind.

But as modern day Christians do we ever ask ourselves if we

are obedient or disobedient in allowing God to mould us? Unless we spend time with the Lord and examine ourselves, we will not know the answer to that question. We know our disobedience stems from Adam and Eve, but do we ever think about it and relate it to our lives?

The best place to start is with the Ten Commandments.

Deuteronomy 5: 1-21 (some verses are abbreviated.)

1. I am the Lord your God – you shall have no other gods before me.

2. You shall not make for yourselves a carved image – any likeness of anything that is in heaven above or is in the earth beneath, or that is in the water under the earth; you shall not bow down to them nor serve them.

3. You shall not take the name of the Lord your God in vain…

4. Observe the Sabbath day, to keep it Holy, as the Lord your God commanded you.

5. Honour your father and your mother.

6. You shall not murder.

7. You shall not commit adultery.

8. You shall not steal.

9. You shall not bear false witness against your neighbour.

10. You shall not covet your neighbour's wife, nor his house, nor his field, or anything that is his neighbours.

The most important is of course the first commandment, that we shall love our God above anything or anyone else. Can we honestly say that we do?

Let us take a look in **Matthew's Gospel 22: 35-40.**

Then one of them, a lawyer, asked Him a question, esting Him, and saying, "Teacher, which is the great commandment in the law?" Jesus said to him. "You shall love the Lord, your God, with all your heart, with all your soul, and with all your mind. This is the first and great commandment. And the second is like it. You shall love your neighbour as yourself. On these two commandments hang all the Law and Prophets."

This brings the question - are we are able to spend 'one hour' with Him, hands free, ears free, minds free, of digital devices?

Matthew 26: 36-46. When Jesus was in the garden of Gethsemane and He asked His disciples to wait a while. **"Sit here while I go and pray over there."**

On returning He found them sleeping and said to Peter: **"What! Could you not watch with Me one hour? Watch** and pray, lest you enter into temptation. The Spirit indeed is willing but the flesh is weak." It happened again, and then again and He said to them. **"Are you still sleeping and resting?"**

Today, perhaps Jesus would ask:

"What! Are you still on your mobiles; still sending texts? Anticipating messages and calls? Watch and pray lest you enter into temptation. Could you not watch with Me for one hour? The Spirit is indeed willing, but the flesh is weak."

And when it comes to loving our neighbours, this does not mean that we embrace their sin. This is not being self-righteous, but righteous. How are we righteous? We are made righteous through Jesus and His Blood sacrifice, not of ourselves.

Ephesians 2:1-8. For by grace you have been saved through faith, and that not of yourselves; it is a gift of God.

The second commandment is to not make images of other gods and worship them.

Some homes have images of Buddha as do shops which sell them. You may like this image, for whatever reason, but he is an image of a false god. Statues of various saints are scattered in churches and gardens. They are images and are not to prayed to, or worshipped.

Our God is a jealous God.

He says in **Deuteronomy5: 8-9. "You shall not make for yourself a carved image – any likeness of anything that is in heaven above, or that is in the earth beneath, or that is in the water under the earth; you shall not bow down before them. For I, the Lord your God, am a jealous God, visiting the iniquity of the fathers upon the children to the third and fourth generations of those who hate Me, but showing mercy to thousands, to those who love Me and keep my commandments."**

Televisions, in some respects, are worshipped, are they not? It is worth thinking about. Now, one may wonder even more about the smart phone. It is used for so many things, living constantly in the hand, or at the ear.

Our eyes and ears are continually focused on this and other digital devices deliberately used by Satan as a means of distraction He is, as we know, the Father of Lies. "You will become wise, knowing all things," perhaps was whispered into the ears of those who 'invented' the digital world. We are deceived, even by some leaders in our churches, as they are deceived in believing that these modern inventions are an 'aid' in our services. Really? That is a lie and a deception – they are of the world – the Bible is of God, and this is where we must separate ourselves from the things of the world.

Genesis 3 is worth a read.

In **Matthew's Gospel 22:17-21** when the Pharisees asked Jesus if it was lawful to pay taxes to Caesar or not. What did He reply? **"Render unto Caesar the things that are Caesar's and to God the things that are God's."** This says it all. When we go to the Lord's House, we must leave behind, or put away, the worldly things we carry around with us and give as much as we are able to worshipping our God.

We were functioning quite well without the mobile, and now children and adults are plunged into mental health problems more than ever before; children and adults are taking their own lives more than ever before. The world is sinking into deception. The smart phone is taken everywhere, from the bathroom to the bedroom; to the streets, to the shops, to the work place, to the desert, to the cinema, to the theatre; to the café, to the restaurant; to the w.c. to the car, to the bus, to the train, to the plane; it is a 'must have', it is a 'can't be without' – not even for 'one hour.' There is less eye contact in surgeries, supermarkets and with folk generally. People in the street are heads down with fingers pressing buttons, not noticing others or simply ignoring them. Family groups seated together are either plugged in or engaged in sending and receiving texts. Vocabulary has become limited. These gadgets maybe here to stay, but let us be wise and discerning as to their use. If we need wisdom, what are we told to do? We ask for it.

James 1:5 tells us that: **If any of you lack wisdom, let him ask of God, who gives to all liberally and without reproach, and it will be given to him. But let him ask in faith, with no doubting for he who doubts is like a wave of the sea driven and tossed by the wind....**

We all need to not just think how we use modern devices, but how much of our time do we give to them? And all the Lord is asking for is just 'one hour' to be with Him; to leave everything else aside. And this 'one hour' is usually where Christians are gathered together in their churches. (There are other 'one hours' in our private lives as well.) If congregations in churches were without smart phones and used their Bibles, it would be a different scenario. There are some who will no doubt say - but that's old fashioned, we need to move with the times.

God is 'old fashioned', in that his laws never change and nor does He. We need to learn to let go of this addiction (for that's what it is) of being continually alert for our phones and afraid of missing calls and texts, when we need to set our minds on Him when we attend church to spend 'one hour' in prayer, worship and listening.

Colossians 3:2 Set your mind on things above, not on things on the earth.

Now to the Third Commandment. You shall not take the name of the Lord God in vain.

This one is disobeyed continually, mostly by unbelievers, but unfortunately by some believers, who appear to be unaware of their use of God's precious name. We need to wake up and be aware. The blasphemy on the television and on radio is frequent. Apparently it is on Face book as well. Our God's name is Holy, for He is Holy, and He will not be mocked or have His Name used as a swear word. Don't you cringe when hearing His precious Name spoken as a nothing? It is a desecration, and God will not tolerate it. Following on from: **You shall not take the name of your Lord God in vain, is: <u>for the Lord will not hold</u>**

him guiltless who takes His Name in vain. Exodus 20:7 (underlining mine)

It is a good to get into the habit when hearing blasphemy, to praise His name. Heads may turn!

Now the 4th Commandment - keeping the Sabbath Day Holy.

This has been disobeyed more so since Sunday trading came into force in the 20th century. The majority of Christians do not regard Sunday shopping as disobeying God's Commandment to keep His day Holy. Remember we are to be set apart.

In 2 Corinthians 17 Paul quotes **Isaiah 52:11** saying, **"Come out from among them and be separate..."**

We need wisdom and discernment here, as we are also to be among unbelievers to tell them about their salvation. Again Paul says, this time in **Romans 10:14-15 How then shall they call on Him in whom they have not believed? And how shall they hear without a preacher? And how shall they preach unless they are sent?**

Ah! **We read in Isaiah 52:7 How beautiful are the feet of those who preach the gospel of peace who bring glad tidings of good things.** It maybe a good idea to read to the end of the chapter.

There are those who do honour His day. Those who honour Him, He will honour. **John 12:26. "If anyone serves Me, let him follow Me; and where I am, there My servant will be also. If anyone serves Me, Him My Father will honour."**

If we take a look at **Isaiah 58:13** we will find this very explicit.

"If you turn your foot from the Sabbath, from doing your pleasure on My Holy day and call the Sabbath a delight, the Holy day of the Lord honourable, and shall honour Him not doing your own ways nor finding your own pleasure, nor speaking your own words then you shall delight yourself in the Lord."

We are to honour our parents is No. 5. Honour your father and mother. What does this mean to 'honour them'? It means to respect them, to love them, to help them, remembering them as, not only those who brought us into this world, but as our seniors.

We are not to murder anyone is No.6. We do, do we not, commit murder in our hearts, as when Jesus says in **Matthew 5:28** with regard to adultery. **"But I say to you**

that whoever looks at a woman to lust for her has already committed adultery with her in his heart." So, too, this has to apply to murder. When in thinking murderous thoughts and wishing someone dead. No?

No.7. We shall not commit adultery. The above encompasses that!

No.8. You shall not steal – if not physically, we often steal in many other ways - another's peace by our lack of love, our criticisms, our nagging, our lies.

Often unkind words are said about another that are not true. This is the meaning of 'bearing false witness' - No.9. We must watch those tongues of ours.

As James writes in his epistle **James 1:26 If anyone among you thinks he is religious, and does not bridle his tongue but deceives his own heart, this one's religion is useless.**

And again in **3:8 No man can tame the tongue. It is an unruly evil, full of deadly poison.**

Now to the last of the ten, telling us not to covet things that we like, belonging to others. We might be envious of those who have more money than us and can afford more material things; perhaps we despise them quietly in our hearts. We must learn to be pleased for them; to look at our own blessings, which can become minimised in our eyes by our covetous feelings.

Hopefully our thinking has been refreshed on the Ten Commandments which God <u>demands</u> us to <u>obey</u>. If we ignore His demands, we do so to our detriment, and we need to wake up, and wake up in a hurry. What once was a Christian nation has turned its back on God. Perhaps it is because God has become a figment of one's imagination; maybe people now think that He has never really existed.

"We were brought up to believe in Him, never really questioning His existence. If He is around, then His laws are old fashioned; He needs to move with the times, after all this is the 21st century; we are free to do what we like, and why not? Men have invented all sorts of devices for us to trust in and men are intelligent beings, so why bother about a supposed God that doesn't bother about the problems of the world; after all, if He is a God of Love, why the child abuse, the disasters, the pain and agony of life generally? If there is a loving God, these things wouldn't happen."

Have we forgotten that we have a free will, which we do have control over if we want to. Plus the fact that we live in a fallen world, which should remind us that My Kingdom is not of this world. The trust in man is so prevalent today and we are warned against it.

Jeremiah 17:5 Thus says the Lord; "cursed is the man that trusts in man, and makes flesh his arm, and whose heart departs from the Lord."

In **Acts 5:29 Then Peter and the other apostles answered and said, "We ought to obey God rather than men."**

It would be good to read the chapters and verses so as to bring the verse into perspective.

Jesus is the same yesterday, today and forever – Hebrews 13: 8

There is no changing with Him.

How wonderful to know and believe that Jesus doesn't change, that He is absolutely steadfast and totally reliable in everything. What a comfort to those who believe in Him.

For some it is so much easier to go along with pleasing man as it saves so much stress. There are 'yes' people in every sphere of life, and in some situations, if you are not one of them, then you are not very popular.

It's less demanding to fall in with the crowd; it saves arguments and keeps the peace. Agreed. Then there is the keeping silent. Is silence golden? Jesus was often silent, especially with Pontius Pilot. However, if we find ourselves in a situation where someone is treating God with disrespect, do we have a duty to say something?

Due to Adam and Eve's disobedience, we are where we are now.

Genesis 2:16 And the Lord God took the man and put him in the garden of Eden to tend and keep it. And the Lord God commanded the man, saying, "Of every tree of the garden you may freely eat; but of the tree of the knowledge of good and evil you shall not eat, for in the day that you eat of it you shall surely die."

Genesis 3:6 …When the woman saw that the tree was good for food, that it was pleasant to the eyes, and a tree desirable to make one wise, she took of its fruit and ate. She also gave to her husband with her and he ate.

If they found it impossible to obey God's one instruction – not to eat of the Tree of Life – how do we cope with the Ten Commandments, plus other rules we read about in the New Testament? The answer lies in: **We can do all things through Christ who strengthens us. Philippians 4:13.**

The world is our oyster; it is full of tasty delicacies, dangling temptations to which it is easier to give into than to resist. Resistance requires effort; it requires stamina, it requires discipline – it requires obedience. Sin requires none of the above, and simply offers enjoyment – be it brief.

As Christians, our safest way is to *"Turn your eyes upon Jesus, look into His Wonderful Face, and the things of earth will grow strangely dim in the light of His glory and grace."* (Lyrics by Helen Howarth Lemmel - 1863-1961) We need to remember **Colossians 3:2 Set your mind on things above, not on things on the earth.**

Our strength, as believers in Christ, lays – <u>in His Word</u>. He promises that He will never leave or forsake us.

Hebrews 13:5-6. Let your conduct be without covetousness; be content with such things as you have. For He Himself has said, "I will never leave you nor forsake you." So we may boldly say "The Lord is my helper; I will not fear. What can man do to me?"

Man is driven by his earthly desires to look to the world and be a part of it. In **1John 2: 15-16** we read: **Do not love the world or the things of the world. If anyone loves the world, the love of the Father is not in him. For all that is in the world – the lust of the flesh, the lust of the eyes,**

and the pride of life – is not of the Father but is of the world. And let us remember **v.17 And the world is passing away, and the lust of it; but he who does the will of God abides forever. Little children, it is the last hour; and as you have heard that the Antichrist is coming, even now many anti-christs have come, by which we know that it is the last hour…**

Romans 5:18 Therefore, as through one man's offence judgement came to all men, resulting in condemnation, even so through one Man's righteous act the free gift came to all men resulting in justification of life.

The first man was of course Adam, who through him sin came into the world; and the second Man was Jesus, who took man's sin onto the cross and forgave us. We have no need to do penance, we cannot atone for our sins in any way; we must repent of them and give our lives to Him who died so that we might be set free. Jesus atoned for our sins.

So, how do we love God? We love Him by obeying Him. We need to ask ourselves if we put Him before our smart phones, Face book, Ipods, Ipads and all the apps that are now available for our use.

Let us search out our hearts and really know deep within

ourselves if we put God before all these worldly things. We can do this searching often during the ONE HOUR we afford the Lord and ourselves.

Psalm 139 makes a wonderful read. **Verses 23-24** is a glorious prayer. **Search me O God; And know my heart; try me, and know my anxieties; and see if there is any wicked way in me, and lead me in the way everlasting.**

It would be excellent to return to using our Bibles, rather than the smart phone Bible app. Not only when we attend church services, but in our prayer groups, Bible studies and private prayer. Bibles have been printed for us to read, to study and to love. We have to be different, and where to share that difference surely has to be within the Body of Christ, when we can step out of the world for one hour.

LONELINESS

Though loneliness may engulf many of us, and more so in these latter days, it is a wonderful opportunity which God has, in His mercy, permitted, as a time to reflect, to focus. A time to turn our hearts and our minds to Him, who said that we are to love Him with all our hearts, our minds and souls. It is a time to learn to forget ourselves, time to become separate, to be, time to 'come out from among them', time to stretch our thinking of what we really are about.

He will never give us more than we are able to bear, as we can read in **1Corinthians 10:13** with regard to temptation….**But God is faithful, who will never allow you to be tempted beyond what you are able, but with the temptation, will also make the way of escape, that you may be able to bear it.**

We also know that He will never leave us or forsake us. In **Deuteronomy 31:6** when Joshua was appointed the new leader of Israel, and no doubt the Israelites were nervous and afraid of the enemy, Moses spoke to him encouragingly, saying – **Be strong and of good courage, do not fear nor be**

afraid of them for the Lord your God, He is the one who goes with you. He will not leave your nor forsake you.... (Be encouraged to read on). So bearing this in mind, and believing that He is our strength and shield, we must try to let go all that we put our reliance on. (Even friends and families.)

Fellowship with others is always recommended, and is important. By nature we are social creatures, and as God says **"It is not good that man should be alone. I will make him a helper comparable to him." Genesis 2:18.**

Nevertheless, we have been, and perhaps are alone, and worse, feel lonely, and it is very painful. God has a reason for everything He allows, or dis-allows in our lives, and if we view it this way, we hopefully, will be able to find purpose in our loneliness. To be alone when feeling lonely is a terrible loneliness, when one may long for the company of another human being, especially someone with whom we have much in common.

To quote C. S. Lewis - 'Oh for the people who speak the same language.' Lewis was not lonely socially, but as a writer, he so needed those who understood him and his writings. His was a loneliness of one kind.

Charles Williams, also a writer, though more famous for his poetry, and a friend of Lewis and a member of The Inklings, a club formed by Lewis whilst at Oxford University. He and his friends would meet once a week in the Bird and Baby, a local pub, where they would share their writings aloud with one another. To quote Williams: 'Much was possible to a man in solitude, but some things are possible only to a man in companionship, and of these, the most important was balance. No mind was so good it did not need another mind to counter and equal it and to save it from conceit and bigotry and folly.'

One more quote, this time by the famous philosopher, writer and much more, Jean-Paul Sartre: 'If you're lonely when you are alone, you're in bad company.' Maybe you have thought, or think the same way, and one can understand this thinking. But, if we know Jesus, then we also know that we are never alone, although it is spiritual company, it is crucial that we recognise it. It is certainly not bad company. Sartre was obviously not a believer, and one can understand non-believers not knowing this wonderful Truth, as they are not born of the Spirit of God, which as believers, we know enables us to understand the Christian way of viewing, and indeed, living.

We read in Luke 5:16 that: So He Himself often withdrew into the wilderness and prayed.

One might say, 'But His circumstances were different; He had to withdraw and be by Himself as the crowds were overwhelming Him'. This was so, and I am sure many of us have experienced having to 'get away' from others, just needing to be alone.

But Jesus knows and understands our feelings of loneliness when we don't want to be alone, but have no option but to be so. He does enter into our circumstances with us, and we can experience this by just 'being', just settling into His spiritual company for a time each day. The rest of the time, we hopefully encounter that 'peace that surpasses all understanding', which we can read about in **Philippines 4:5-7 Let your gentleness be known to all men. The Lord is at hand. Be anxious for nothing, but in everything by prayer and supplication, with thanksgiving, let your requests be made known to God; and <u>the peace of God, which surpasses all understanding, will guard your hearts and minds through Christ Jesus</u>.** (underlining mine)

How many Christians would be able to be on their own without their smart phones, iPads, iPods, tablets, television, and other paraphernalia of the digital age, all switched off for any length of time, and not just in their homes, but whilst attending church, meetings, visiting family, friends, out shopping, walking? The vast majority would not even consider it. Consequently, they can never be alone. Many, however, might experience loneliness.

It is vital to be able to switch off from the world for a period of time each day. That is to switch off our digital gadgets, and to switch off our minds from the world's way of thinking. God's thoughts are not our thoughts, nor His ways our ways.

Isaiah 55:6-8 tells us. Seek the Lord while He may be found, call upon Him while He is near. Let the wicked forsake his ways, and the unrighteous man his thoughts. Let him return to the Lord, and He will have mercy on him, and to our God, for He will abundantly pardon. "<u>For my thoughts are not your thoughts, nor are your ways my ways</u>," says the Lord. "<u>For as the heavens are higher than the earth, so are my ways higher than your ways, and my thoughts than your thoughts</u>." (underlining mine)

God's ways maybe not our ways, nor His thoughts our thoughts, but we can, by spending time with Him, get to know much about Him. The loneliness we experience can really be put to good use. We have the opportunity to seek Him while He may be found and we can call upon Him whilst He is near. We need to take advantage of the opportunities He avails us, and use them for our sakes and for His glory.

It is so easy to bemoan our circumstances, and yes, even though we are Christians, we are still very human. So was Moses, so was Joseph, so was Elijah, so was David, so was Peter, all who suffered from loneliness, but through their experience had real and worthwhile relationships with their God.

We must remember too, that Jesus suffered terribly from loneliness. Yes, He was divine, but He took on our humanity so as He could relate to us in ours. We do not have to be a Moses or a Peter, we just have to be ourselves. It is fine to look to these people of God as wonderful examples, but we are who God made us to be, and comparisons are not necessarily helpful.

Let us refuse to compare ourselves with others allowing them to make us feel inadequate, but rather allowing them to encourage us is more helpful. This goes for most things in life. If we have a personal relationship with Jesus, it doesn't belong to anyone else; it is His and your friendship, no-one else's. We look at life through different eyes because we are different in so many areas – our circumstances, our backgrounds, education, nationalities, the way we speak – all these make us unique and individual.

However, our sameness is a belief in a wonderful God and Saviour. We read the same words in His Book, believe them, acknowledge them, and in this we are one in fellowship. If we seek My Kingdom first, everything else shall be added unto us. **Matthew 6:33 "But seek first the kingdom of God and His righteousness, and all these things shall be added unto you."** And not just material things; most importantly, peace, patience, integrity, understanding and all the other necessary accessories we need in our lives. He gives us His company when we are craving for human company, and if that isn't enough, He might send a phone call, a letter, an email, or even a caller, just to reassure us that we are never really alone, despite the fact that we are feeling extremely lonely.

It is horrible, and a destructive feeling if we allow it to get the better of us, one which can lead to depression and even suicide. Judas, who betrayed our Lord must have felt such a terrible loneliness, thus he took his own life. We must not allow ourselves to reach this point.

Hebrews 13:5-6 Let your conduct be without

covetousness and be content with such things as you have. For He Himself has said. "I will never leave you nor forsake you." So we may boldly say: "The Lord is my helper; I will not fear. What can man do to me?"

Spring, summer and autumn days can be just as lonely as the dark, dismal, wet and cold days of winter. It is not the weather, but our minds, our thinking, that puts us in the doldrums of loneliness. Our minds are like land mines, once trodden on, explode, causing untold damage.

Satan is master of this world. We always need to remember this. Jesus says in **John 18:36 "My kingdom is not of this world. If my kingdom were of this world, my servants would fight, so that I should not be delivered to the Jews, but my kingdom is not from here."** (It is usually a good idea to read the proceeding verse or verses so as to understand the full measure of what is being said.)

In knowing this, and learning to keep our eyes on Jesus, looking into His wonderful face, the things of earth growing strangely dim in the light of His glory and grace.

O soul are you weary and troubled?
No light in the darkness you see?
There's light for a look at the Saviour
And life more abundant and free.

Turn your eyes upon Jesus
Look into His wonderful face
And the things of earth will grow strangely dim
In the light of His glory and grace.

His word shall not fail you, He promised,
Believe Him and all will be w ell,
Then go to a world that is dying
His perfect salvation to tell.
(Helen H. Lemmel 1922-1961)

And in **Hebrews 12:2….looking unto Jesus, the author and finisher of our faith, who for the joy that was set before Him endured the cross, despising the shame, and has sat down at the right hand of the throne of God.**

It is so very easy to become despondent, allowing loneliness to take over our lives. It is a struggle, one doesn't deny this, and whatever the circumstances under which one is living, it is so important to know – **That there is no condemnation in Christ Jesus, who do not walk according to the flesh, but according to the Spirit. Romans 8:1.**

When we are deprived of human company, being lonely

can push us into a one way thought process. This is like driving down a narrow one-way street, and not being able to turn back. We become stuck. So, too, we become stuck in a mind set focusing on self, thinking all negative thoughts, forgetting about all the positive, which seem to have disappeared altogether.

STROLLING OUT

No matter what the weather be, to don one's coat and walking shoes, to take a stroll, just has to be worthwhile, one doesn't have to dress in style, just comfort.

A summer's day brings warmth upon the skin and hair and fills the heart with ne'er a care.

Spring is gentle, and one can spy new life peeping through the earth as it gives in birth.

Autumn brings a rush, a flurry, as if the leaves are in a hurry to wave good-bye.

It seems that nature wants to settle down a while as cold takes hold ushering in the winter bold.

To stroll down English country lanes, across the fields as seasons yield their harvest, has to be the best of magic.

It takes away all insulation, stretches mind and body, no

limitation to the pleasures that it brings. One sings aloud or softly hums and finds life easy to succumb to.

Strolling helps one be reflective, can bring one's life into perspective, removes cobwebs of memories, refreshes thinking like a breeze.

Finally:

Isaiah 4:10 Fear not, for I am with you; be not dismayed, for I am your God. I will strengthen you. Yes, I will help you. I will uphold you with My righteous right hand.